MW00653494

An Overview of Contemporary Theories

FEMINIST SOCIOLOGY

JANET SALTZMAN CHAFETZ
UNIVERSITY OF HOUSTON

F.E. PEACOCK PUBLISHERS, INC., Itasca, Illinois

Copyright © 1988
F.E. Peacock Publishers, Inc.
All rights reserved
Library of Congress Catalog
Card Number 87-062-928
ISBN 0-087581-327-5
Printed in the U.S.A.

PREFACE

In the spring of 1985, I sat around a lunch table in Chicago
with several feminist sociologists who bemoaned the paucity of feminist theory in sociology, especially compared to some of our sister disciplines in the
social sciences and humanities (see Stacey and Thorne, 1985). At the time I
was convinced, although I must admit silently, that they were wrong. After
spending a year searching sociological literature for feminist theory, I dis-
covered that my Chicago colleagues were not entirely wrong. I believe that
there is a wealth of feminist commitment in sociology, but several things
mitigate against theory development in our field. The substance of this book
is testimony to the richness of feminist theory; however, a number of the theorists whose ideas are discussed come from other social sciences and are sociologists neither by training nor by affiliation.

Four characteristics of American sociology make theory development
difficult. First, a disproportionate number of feminist sociologists in the past
decade and a half have been in the early stages of their careers, reflecting the
substantial influx of women into the discipline since 1970. To acquire a job,
promotion, and tenure, one must publish copiously, and there is special emphasis on publishing articles in high prestige, general sociological journals.
It is difficult to have a purely theoretical paper accepted in such journals. An
article that reports data will typically have too little room for the full development of a new theoretical idea, given the page limitations of journals.
Moreover, by its very nature original theory tends to be controversial, thus
reducing the probability of its acceptance further. Hence, there is a tendency
among young sociologists to test hypotheses derived from preexisting theory and/or from research literature with some relatively minor alterations or

additions. This has led to a substantial amount of good feminist research, but perhaps hindered theoretical development.

Second, in general there is a paucity of new theory in American sociology. Required courses in theory usually emphasize the ideas of our long-dead, mostly European founders: the so-called classics. "Theory" pieces in our journals tend to endlessly debate, reinterpret, and rehash the ideas of a small number of thinkers — again heavily emphasizing the classics along with some contemporary European thinkers. The focus of the Theory Section of the American Sociological Association has been largely the same. Most American sociologists have not been trained to view theoretical development as an integral part of their work. The result is that "theorists" are typically seen as having their own specialty, one akin to intellectual history or textual exegesis, and others define themselves as "not-theorists." Consequently, the various substantive areas of our discipline are often impoverished in theory (the study of gender may be one of the less impoverished, in fact), while existing theory is often so general that it is difficult to apply to concrete issues. This scarcely constitutes an original insight into the ills of our discipline. It goes back at least to the 1950s and Merton's (1957) call for theories of the middle range. I think it remains a valid point.

Third, it appears to me that feminist sociologists are disproportionately committed to those sociological perspectives such as Ethnomethodology, Symbolic Interactionism, and Marxism, which in general tend to focus most heavily on the description and analysis of concrete processes or specific historical eras. There is thus much more descriptive material available to document sexism than there are general theoretical efforts to understand it.

Finally, and perhaps most importantly, American sociology, including feminist sociology, continues to be substantially ethnocentric and time bound. Our research is overwhelmingly conducted in the contemporary United States, and except for some macrosociologists, is rarely comparative. I have argued in another context (Chafetz and Dworkin, 1986: chapter 2) that the development of theoretical explanations requires historical and cross-cultural comparison. Such comparison enables us to distinguish between relatively widespread or uniform explanatory variables and processes and idiosyncratic phenomena. Since cultural anthropology is a fundamentally comparative social science, it is not surprising that it is richer than sociology in feminist theory. Nonetheless, there is now a substantial amount of good feminist theory written by sociologists, as well as theory directly relevant to the work of sociologists written by others.

Almost every year at the annual meetings of the American Sociological Association, the Sex and Gender Section runs a session dealing with "feminist theory." It is one of the best attended regular sessions during the entire five-day meeting. Afterwards, around the corridors and in the restaurants, restrooms and bars, one hears the term "feminist theory" constantly. Obviously, there is a lot of interest in the topic. Yet there is no book that reviews and summarizes the variety of contemporary feminist theories in sociology, despite a number of activist, philosophical, anthropological, and historical readers and books dealing with feminist theory. There is no place where we can send our students for an introduction to this increasingly rich and varied literature. There is no place where we can read up on the topic preparatory to lecturing to our students. There is no place where we can easily explore the many theoretical options we might be able to use in our own research work.

This book is the first step in rectifying that situation. It presents an overview of the major types of feminist theory in sociology or directly useful to sociologists that have emerged since about 1970. It is written so that it can be read by undergraduates who have not necessarily studied general sociological theory. However, I also hope that more advanced students and professionals (in the roles of both teacher and researcher) will find it a useful starting point or summary.

I have chosen an unorthodox format for a theory book. I have organized theoretical perspectives around four broad substantive issues: the causes of gender inequality, mechanisms that maintain systems of gender inequality, the consequences of such systems, and processes of change in them. In organizing the material this way rather than around people or schools of thought, I hope to de-emphasize individuals and the detailed textual exegesis of individual works, which I think is a rather sterile exercise for sociologists. Rather, I hope to demonstrate how diverse theoretical approaches can be valuable tools in our attempt to understand specific empirical issues. I have undoubtedly omitted theoretical issues, works, and individuals that others would choose to include. The potentially relevant literature is vast and the dividing point between theoretical and empirical work not always as clear as one might suppose. Certainly, given that this book is designed to be an overview accessible to undergraduates, no theories will be treated in great depth.

I would like to express my gratitude to the Center for Public Policy of the College of Social Sciences and to the Sociology Department of the University of Houston, Central Campus, for their support of this project. The former provided research expenses, the latter secretarial assistance and a much-needed research assistant. Lonnie Anderson and Mary Jo Duncan provided excellent and cheerful word processing, for which I am grateful. To research assistant, Maryvonne Lorenzen, go my heartiest thanks for an arduous and well-done bibliographic search. Further bibliographic help was provided by another student, Renee Barton. Helen Rose Ebaugh, Joseph Kotarba, A. Gary Dworkin, Elizabeth Almquist, and Ruth Wallace read and commented on a completed draft. Their comments were very helpful and their encouragement well appreciated. Finally, I am grateful to my friend and publisher, Ted Peacock, for his enthusiasm for this project and his faith in my ability to do it.

Janet Saltzman Chafetz
Houston, Texas

CONTENTS

3 MAINTENANCE AND REPRODUCTION OF GENDER SYSTEMS / 67

Contents   xi

4 SOCIAL CONSEQUENCES OF GENDER STRATIFICATION / 115

5 CHANGING SYSTEMS OF GENDER INEQUALITY / 127

| INTRODUCTION

Feminist Sociology: An Overview of Contemporary Theories is a survey of the varieties of contemporary (since about 1970) sociological thought that could reasonably be subsumed under the rubric of feminist theory. I hope to present the array of feminist theoretical approaches in sociology and our sister disciplines that can be of direct use to sociologists in their attempts to understand the complex relationships between gender and a host of social phenomena. The book, however, is not designed to be an in-depth or definitive treatment of feminist sociological theory.

Among sociologists who share an interest in the study of gender, there is widespread consensus that there are many types of feminist theory. Just as there is little agreement as to what constitutes sociological theory, there is not much consensus on what feminist theory is. It is also not always very clear what distinguishes feminist theory from other theories dealing with gender issues.

I generally view the study of theory in the same light as many view sociological methods: as a diverse set of practical tools from which we can select those most helpful in solving any given intellectual or practical problem. The more tools we have at our disposal, the more adequately we can understand that which we seek to understand. My goal is to direct sociologists towards an understanding of which theoretical approaches are best suited for which issues so that they can synthesize and combine those that are useful in studying a given topic. This process requires that each theory be critically assessed. However, I have chosen not to explore the empirical, logical, and conceptual shortcomings, often extensively discussed and debated in the literature, of the theories reviewed. I will concentrate on simply presenting concise, and I hope unbiased, accounts of the theories selected.

THEORY

In this book, "theory" will mean any systematic attempt to *understand* or *explain*: to answer questions of why, how, or what the consequences are of a given phenomenon. Sociological theory is integrally related to research; it functions to explain that which we know — or can know — empirically about the social world. In this sense, theory is amenable to empirical testing and potential falsification. Excluded from consideration, therefore, are inherently untestable philosophical and normative discussions of gender. I have also excluded discussions that are simply critiques of the works of others, epistemological discussions concerning how feminists ought to go about constructing theories, and works that are basically empirical descriptions or tests of empirical hypotheses.

Just as sociology has, in recent years, witnessed an outpouring of research and theory concerning gender, so too have the other social and behavioral sciences (especially psychology and anthropology) and the humanities (especially philosophy, history, literature, and linguistics). Although these disciplines contribute in fundamental ways to our understanding of gender and society, it is beyond the scope of this book to review all of their contributions. While my focus will be primarily sociological, social scientific theories from other disciplines will be included. The bases of selection for these theories are three: (1) they reflect a specific sociological theoretical tradition; (2) I have judged them to be potentially quite useful to the work of feminist sociologists; or (3) they have been widely cited in the sociological literature. In particular, a number of feminist anthropological theories are included.

Sociology and anthropology fundamentally concern themselves with the same broad issues, especially in terms of those that constitute the focus of this book, although they differ to some extent theoretically and methodologically. By and large, sociologists study more complex societies, anthropologists simpler, often preliterate, peasant or tribal ones. The theories of each are often used by the other. Feminist anthropological data, concepts, and theories have been especially influential in the development of recent macrolevel feminist thought in sociology. Many feminist social psychological theories have been strongly influenced by theory and research in the fields of psychology and psychoanalysis. These fields are also well represented in the discussions of microlevel theory throughout the book.

In each of the remaining four chapters one basic issue will be examined from the perspectives of several theoretical traditions. First, analyses of the *causes* of gender inequality (sex stratification, patriarchy, sexism, male dominance, female oppression) will be reviewed. Next, explanations of the *mechanisms that maintain* systems of gender inequality will be covered. Third, discussions of the nongender-related *consequences* of gender differentiation and inequality will be considered. Finally, I will end with a review of approaches to the activist issue of how *change* toward greater gender equality can be brought about.

In selecting these four theoretical issues, I have obviously ignored many more that could have been addressed. My intent in this book is to make clear the range of theoretical approaches available to contemporary feminist sociologists. I have chosen four issues that seem to me collectively to accomplish several goals. First, they provide ample opportunity to sample the full range of approaches. Second, they allow for the juxtaposition of differing approaches to the same issues. Third, they are quite general, and therefore potentially applicable both cross-culturally and historically. Fourth, they refer to empirically observable phenomena. Finally, to me they all represent the quintessentially *sociological* level of analysis: the structure, or patterned regularities, of social phenomena. Indeed, these issues can be viewed as the gendered version of what have been, since the inception of our discipline, four of the most fundamental and frequently addressed general theoretical issues: the origins of social structural features, especially systems of inequality; the consequences (functions) of such structures; mechanisms that reproduce the status quo; and mechanisms that change the status quo.

Feminist theoretical approaches to the four issues raised can be roughly divided into two types: macrostructural and microinteractional. The microlevel refers to face-to-face interactions between people and those types of groups, such as the family and peer group, in which such interactions occur. The macrolevel refers to larger social groupings in which relationships are secondary or indirect; these include formal organizations, the polity, economy, and society itself. I also include in the macrolevel broadly agreed upon social definitions such as those embodied in religions, ideologies, and social norms. The macrostructural includes feminist versions of Marxian analysis and several anthropological and eclectic sociological theories. By eclectic I mean theories that are neither rooted in, nor represent explicit revisions or expansions of, any specific general social theories. The microinteractional approaches include feminist versions derived from Psychoanalytic theory; from the Symbolic Interaction and Ethnomethodological orientations, which for simplicity will be collectively grouped under the rubric of the "Everyday Life approach"; and from Cognitive Developmental and Social Learning theories, which will be collectively considered as the "Socialization approach." Feminist versions of Role theory and Exchange theory are also included. Each of these has microinteractional as well as macrostructural variants. I do not mean to suggest that there is complete homogeneity within each of these categories of feminist theory, nor within the general theoretical traditions that they reflect. There is both diversity within and overlap between them. Nonetheless, I find that by using this particular scheme to categorize and discuss the various theories, I can maximize my coverage of them without unnecessarily complicating the discussion.

None of the various feminist theories addresses all four gender inequality issues. Most deal with one or two as their central concern, and at most address the others in a peripheral, sometimes only implicit, manner. The causes of gender inequality are addressed primarily by macrostructural theories. Mechanisms that maintain the status quo comprise the central focus of microinteractional theories, although many macrostructural theories are focused on this issue. Both general theory types may include discussions of the consequences of gender inequality, but most often do not. Finally, while by definition social change is a concern and commitment for all feminist theorists (as will be explained shortly), the ability of the various theoretical formulations to adequately explain mechanisms of change or to provide *theoretically derived* strategies to expedite change is variable within both broad categories of theory.

In this chapter I will briefly review several general theoretical traditions that serve as background for the particular feminist versions to be discussed in later chapters. However, before turning to that, I will discuss what, precisely, I mean by "feminist theory."

FEMINIST THEORY

The first time I heard the term "feminist theory" in the context of sociology was about 1974 or 1975. My response was to deny even the possibility of its existence. Since for me theory in any science is an attempt to explain or understand some aspect of the empirical world, I could not understand what might be the subject matter of something called feminist theory. Over the ensuing years it became increasingly evident to me that there is indeed no *one* thing that can be called feminist theory. It became equally clear, however, that a number of theories being developed reflected a feminist consciousness — an awareness rooted in a commitment to activist goals. My perception that feminist theory constitutes a radically new way of understanding the social world remained vague and undefined until I decided to write this book. Before I faced the issue of what to include or exclude from the book, I had to clarify for myself what, exactly, makes a theory of some aspect(s) of the social world a *feminist* social theory.

All social theories have political ramifications, whether or not these are explicitly spelled out by the theorist. When carefully examined, it becomes apparent that the logical conclusion to be drawn from a given theory is that social change is either desirable or not, that social change can or cannot be brought about by willful human effort. The very issues raised by any theory reflect a political stance, as do its underlying assumptions concerning human nature, the nature of society, the process of social change, and so on.

Since the inception of sociology in the nineteenth century, theorists have often dealt (albeit usually only in passing) with issues pertaining to sex and gender. Clearly, not all—or even most—of these have been informed by a feminist consciousness. Indeed, many are antithetical to feminist goals and values. There is an extensive literature, developed since about 1970, that criticizes traditional theoretical approaches on feminist grounds. Closely related to this literature, often interwoven with it, has been a growing epistemological literature dealing with what theories and methods ought to be like when informed by a feminist perspective (e.g., Farganis, 1986; Kasper, 1986; the various articles in Millman and Kanter, 1975; Acker, 1973; Oakley, 1974). Some of these works (e.g., Cook and Fonow, 1986; Mies, 1983; Westcott, 1979) claim that a feminist sociology must involve "praxis." That is, the feminist sociologist should be involved in changing society, raising feminist consciousness, and working to reduce gender inequality, in the very process of doing sociology.

I do not accept this extreme an activist definition of feminist sociology or theory. The central task of any science and its theories is to aid in our understanding or explanation of some class of empirical phenomena. Improved understanding can often result in better means to change phenomena, but the activist role is not inherent in the intellectual enterprise per se. Rather, the acid test of whether a theory is feminist for purposes of this book rests with whether it *can be used* (regardless of by whom) to challenge, counteract, or change a status quo that disadvantages or devalues women. It is a judgement of the theory itself, not of the scholar(s) who created it. Conversely, a theory that can be used to support such a status quo is not a feminist theory, regardless of its subject matter or author(s).

There are three specific elements, in addition to the acid test, which I think render a theory feminist, and thus appropriate for inclusion in this book. First, *gender comprises a central focus or subject matter* of the theory. Feminist theory seeks ultimately to understand the gendered nature of virtually all social relations, institutions, and processes. Second, *gender relations are viewed as a problem*. By this I mean that feminist theory seeks to understand how gender is related to social inequities, strains, and contradictions. Finally, *gender relations are not viewed as either natural or immutable*. Rather, the gender-related status quo is viewed as the product of sociocultural and historical forces which have been created, and are constantly re-created by humans, and therefore can potentially be changed by human agency.

Perhaps more than most sociological theories, feminist theories tend to be explicitly political in inspiration and in their advocacy of social change. This in itself does not, however, reduce their explanatory power. The political consciousness fostered by feminism has produced a generation of sociologists who are asking questions heretofore largely ignored, offering insights and understandings otherwise impossible to glean, and expanding our understanding of social life to include the previously invisible female half of the population. As stated by Roslyn Bologh (1984:382), "Feminist theorizing promises not only to fill the gaps in knowledge about women but to provide an alternative perception of the world that men, because of their (dominant) position, could not possess." The politics of feminist theories are only more self-conscious and explicit, not more intrusive or biasing, than those of most other theories.

CLASSICAL THEORETICAL ORIENTATIONS: AN OVERVIEW

The rest of this introduction presents a brief discussion of the general theories that are springboards for the feminist theories included in the next four chapters. I will focus on two aspects of these theories: (1) an explanation of their overall approach in very general terms; and (2) an account of those specifics required to understand material covered later in the book. These reviews are not an exegesis of the full range of ideas and concepts developed by the theories, and therefore do not substitute for the more general and detailed treatments to be found in standard theory texts.

MARX AND ENGELS

The importance of classical Marxist theory for feminist theory is twofold. On the one hand, there are those theorists who explicitly call themselves Marxist-feminists, who have attempted to broaden classical Marxism to account for gender inequality adequately. These theorists do not abandon the Marxian emphases on capitalism as the source of contemporary inequalities and the necessity of bringing about a classless society in order to rectify inequalities, including that based on gender. The Marxist-feminists typically take as a major point of departure the essay by Friedrich Engels, Marx's collaborator, *The Origin of the Family, Private Property and the State* (first published in 1884).

On the other hand, there are a variety of theorists whose ideas about gender inequality and social change are rooted in the underlying logic of Marxist theory, which is generally termed **dialectical materialism**. These theorists do not consider themselves Marxist-feminists, nor do they necessarily assume that the existence of capitalism or its demise constitute central issues of importance to their analysis of gender systems and their change. Those feminist theorists inspired by Marx's underlying theoretical logic do not typically begin from any one source.

I will begin this overview of Marxist theory with a discussion of dialectical materialism, then move to Marx's analysis of capitalism, followed by a review of Engels's essay, and end with a short discussion of a contemporary offshoot of Marxist theory known as World Systems analysis.

Dialectical Materialism

Materialism refers to a philosophical assumption (the opposite of which is philosophical **idealism**) that argues that the material realities of human life shape the ways in which people think about and structure their collective existence. Specifically, the manner in which people satisfy their needs by acting on the environment (which is their labor) structures their thought systems (ideologies, religions), family relations, systems of social inequality, political and educational systems, and so on. The organization of work is commonly called the economic structure. Materialism can be understood as an approach that looks to economic structure, process, and relations as the key variables in explaining and understanding virtually all other aspects of sociocultural life.

The concept of **dialectic** (which Marx borrowed from Hegel, an idealist philosopher) constitutes a scheme for understanding change. Inherent in a dialectical model of change are two assumptions: that significant change is generated by conflict; and that all systems have within themselves contradictions which ultimately produce conflict, hence change.

The dialectical approach begins with an existing social system, termed a **thesis**. In the hands of a materialist such as Marx, the thesis is, first and foremost, a functioning economic system (called the **infrastructure**), along with the characteristic thought system, family, political, educational, social stratification, and other structures (the **superstructure**) which emanate from and support it. Those people who control the economy and profit from the system constitute the dominant social class.

Since the system contains within itself inherent strains and contradictions, the thesis generates its own opposition, termed the **antithesis**. For Marx, this opposition is a social class which is economically, hence socially, disadvantaged ("oppressed," "exploited") by the existing system and dominant class. To become an oppositional force — an antithesis — the members of the disadvantaged class must become collectively aware of their common interests, and aware of the fact that they share a common enemy in that class which controls and profits from the existing system (the thesis). The oppressed come to understand that their personal problems are in fact collective; that they are rooted in the existing system; and that only radical system change can alleviate them. This awareness Marx called **class consciousness**. In the hands of other theorists, class consciousness has become gender, race, and ethnic consciousness. These concepts, while focusing on a different basis for commonality of interests, maintain the Marxian emphasis on understanding the structural basis of collective disadvantage and the need for collective action in order to change social structure as the mechanism to alleviate disadvantage.

Once in existence, the antithesis (the fully conscious disadvantaged class) engages in conflict with the thesis (the dominant class), the result of which is a completely new socioeconomic system, termed the **synthesis**. In turn, the synthesis becomes a new thesis and the process of historical change begins anew.

Capitalist Systems

Capitalism is that economic system in which the means of production (i.e., those things such as land, tools, machines, factories, and natural resources required for work) are owned by some private individuals. According to Marx, this system emerged as a synthesis after feudalism. The owners of the means of production constitute a social class called the **bourgeoisie**. Their primary interest is to maximize their profits. Most people do not own the means of production. In order to survive, they must sell their labor power to those who do. They constitute the disadvantaged class, called the **proletariat**. The labor they provide to capitalists is termed **social labor**.

In order both to survive the fierce competition with other firms, and to maximize their profits, capitalists pay their workers exploitative wages. From Marx's perspective, the true value of a product is a function of the amount of labor that goes into its production, and essentially nothing else. However, workers are not paid the true value of their work. Rather, they receive wages sufficient only to maintain them at subsistence level and to reproduce a new generation of workers. The difference between such wages and the true value they produce is a measure of their exploitation, and it constitutes the capitalist's profits. That difference is known in Marxist vocabulary as **surplus value**. Since capitalists seek to maximize surplus value, they seek to insure a legally free labor force, one unbound by traditional restrictions that impede the ability of capitalists to seek out the most exploitable people for employment.

Capitalist production is preeminently social, requiring the cooperative labor of many people to produce a product. To Marx, this feature of capitalism constitutes a direct contradiction with the private ownership of the means and products of production by individuals who do not themselves contribute to production. This contradiction, combined with the severe exploitation of workers, forms the base from which develops a class-conscious proletariat—the antithesis to capitalism. The process of consciousness development depends upon substantial contact among members of the disadvantaged class, which, under capitalism, occurs in factories and in urban working class residential districts.

For Marx, the dynamic of dialectical change is specifically class conflict.

He postulates that the synthesis of communism that is to follow the coming demise of capitalism will be a classless society, which will end the dialectic process. Since family structure and relations, as part of the superstructure, reflect the economic base of society, a classless, communist society will, presumably, solve the problem of gender inequality as well. From this perspective, the exploitation of women is a function of an exploitative economic system. Abolishing the latter will automatically serve to abolish the former. It is this assumption that has most troubled Marxist-feminists and prompted their efforts to reformulate Marxism to better account for the oppression of women.

Engels's Theory

Engels developed an evolutionary theory of the family and relative status of women based on Marx's general perspective. He began by dividing human history into three stages: savagery (roughly hunting/gathering societies), barbarianism (roughly horticultural societies), and civilization (beginning with agrarian and pastoral societies and continuing into the present, capitalist era). These three stages each have characteristic forms of marriage: group, pairing, and monogamous. He argued that during the first and most of the second stages, both women and men were free to have multiple sex partners. Since paternity was never known with certainty, descent was reckoned through the mother's lineage. Households were communistic, meaning that several related women, their husbands, and children lived together and shared equally. Women were highly respected and free, the equals to or superiors of men.

During the first two stages, little wealth was produced that could be inherited by children. Human labor power was sufficient to provide for the maintenance of household members, but not to produce a surplus. With the introduction of herding, agriculture, metalworking, and weaving (the dawn of the third stage) came a drastic change in family structure and the status of women. The impetus for change was the creation of inheritable wealth. These new modes of production resulted in surplus, which originally accrued to the woman-centered household and lineage. Engels argued that the familial division of labor that existed up to that time required that men obtain food while women maintained the household (an assertion rejected by contemporary anthropologists). Each sex owned the instruments of labor necessary to its work. "Therefore, according to the social custom of the time, the man was also the owner of the new source of subsistence, the cattle, and later of the new instruments of labour, the slaves" (Engels, 1972:85). In this way, the man's position within the family became more important than the woman's. In turn, men were prompted to overthrow the traditional matrilineal order of inheritance, which left his property to his wife's blood relatives (primarily her nephews). Simply put, men wanted their own sons to inherit their property. In order to insure that it was indeed their own children who inherited, women's sexuality had to be controlled so that paternity could be clearly established. Engels asserted:

> The overthrow of mother right was the *world historical defeat of the female sex.* The man took control in the home . . . ; the woman was degraded and reduced to servitude; she became the slave of his lust and a mere instrument for the production of children. (1972:87; emphasis in the original)

Thus, according to Engels, out of the development of private property came the patriarchal family and monogamous marriage. Since the purpose of monogamy was to ensure paternity, however, only women were forced to be monogamous; men have continued to practice group marriage through adultery and prostitution.

Far from being based on love, monogamous marriage reflected economic considerations, with parents choosing their children's spouse. According to Engels, economic concerns have continued to dominate marriage formation among all ruling classes, including capitalists. He labeled this "the crassest prostitution," noting that

> sometimes . . . both partners, but far more commonly . . . the woman, . . . differs from the ordinary courtesan in that she does not let out her body on piecework as a wage worker, but sells it once and for all into slavery. (1972:102)

However, Engels claimed that romantic love between husbands and wives has been possible in the oppressed classes, including the proletariat. Since there is no property to preserve or inherit, "there is no incentive to make this male supremacy effective" (1972:102). In addition, under capitalism proletariat women often work in factories, thus depriving men of the economic basis of their supremacy. This analysis of the relations and relative equality of the sexes within the working class constitutes an important focus of attack by contemporary Marxist-feminists.

In the first two stages of history, household management was as public and socially necessary a labor as procuring food. As the nuclear, monogamous family developed, household work became private service, and the wife became "head servant, excluded from . . . social production" (1972:104). Barred from social production, women became legally subordinated to men as well.

Engels concluded his general theoretical statement by arguing that the first precondition for women's liberation is "to bring the whole female sex back into public industry," which entails abolishing the monogamous family as an economic unit, and with it the prostitution of women (1972:105-6). This will result from the abolition of capitalism—the private ownership of the means of production—which will also eliminate concerns about inheritance and paternity. Housework and childcare will become social labor again. Under these conditions, monogamy of a different sort will flourish: men and women will freely and equally commit themselves to each other on the basis of love. This assumption, that the demise of capitalism will automatically eliminate women's oppression, constitutes the major focus of criticism leveled against Engels's theory by contemporary Marxist-feminists.

World Systems Theory

World Systems theory is a Marxian-inspired approach developed over the past decade and a half. Beginning in about the sixteenth century in certain areas of western Europe, capitalism has increasingly penetrated other parts of the world, tying more and more societies into an integrated network or system. Within that system there are three types of societies: **core, peripheral,** and **semiperipheral.** Depending on the status of a society in terms of these three types, there are very different ramifications for the local economy and for its sociopolitical structure and relationships.

In any given era, one or a few nations constitute the core of the world system, enjoying world hegemony based on their economic dominance. Core societies have the most advanced, diversified, active, and wealthy economies of their time. They are also characterized by strong, stable governments. Today, such nations as West Germany, Japan, and the United States are part of the core. Peripheral nations have far less wealthy and sophisticated and more labor-intensive economies, which are often specialized around one or a few commodities. They may be colonies, or they have weak, often unstable governments. Many African, Latin American, and Caribbean countries fall in this category. Semiperipheral nations fall between the two extremes and often play an important role as intermediaries between the core and periphery. This type includes today such countries as Saudi Arabia, Argentina, and South Africa.

In their search to maximize profits, capitalists in core nations expand into other societies, seeking cheap, exploitable labor and raw materials, as well as new markets. It is their investment, marketing, and purchasing behavior that largely structures the economies, hence superstructures, of peripheral and semiperipheral nations. For instance, in core nations most workers derive their family income entirely from wage employment. However, in the periphery, and to a lesser extent the semiperiphery, wages are so low and employment so sporadic that large numbers of workers derive only part of their family livelihood from full-time wage employment. They must supplement this with work in the hidden economy of petty trading, handicraft manufacturing and service, or by small-scale horticulture or agriculture. As capitalism increasingly expands in a nation, traditional modes of production often decline or are lost, while the new modes leave most people impoverished. A new, but small, indigenous bourgeoisie also develops. In this way, the class structure is altered, with profound cultural, political, and social ramifications.

In general, World Systems theory is an attempt to expand Marxist analysis to explicitly recognize and systematically include the impact of capitalist development on the entire world. A major contribution of this theory to the classical Marxist approach is the recognition that capitalism affects the social structure of nations very differently, depending on the status of a nation within the world economic system. Feminists working from this perspective take it one step further by examining and explaining the differential impact of national economic status on men and women.

Summary

Contemporary Marxist-feminists maintain the focus of classical and neo-Marxist theory on capitalist systems and the impact of this particular economic form on social relations and structure. This leads them to emphasize the distinction and relationship between social labor for wages that produces surplus value and private, nonwage labor for domestic units. They depart most strikingly from other Marxists — past and present — by rejecting the idea that the demise of capitalism will automatically bring about gender equality. Rather, borrowing from other feminist approaches, they argue that patriarchy, that is, male domination, constitutes an analytically and historically distinct system that has been affected by and has affected economically based class systems. Men and women of the proletariat (and the bourgeoisie as well) do not share complete commonality of interest because of the interpenetration of capitalism and patriarchy. Their analyses are thus heavily focused on how these two systems, each of which modifies and supports the other, combine to produce historically specific forms of female oppression. The oppression of women is both different from, and greater than, that of male proletariats. Logically, then, solutions to the problem of oppression are not identical for the two sexes either.

MAX WEBER

Several of the feminist theories discussed in later chapters call upon either the general theoretical orientation developed by Max Weber in direct reaction against Marx's approach, or on his analyses of social status and power.

In discussing Marx's concept of the dialectic, I mentioned that the opposite of philosophical materialism is idealism. Weber was an idealist. For him, collective systems of thought, especially religious understandings and interpretations of the world, constitute the basis out of which social and economic structures grow. Individuals behave in ways that have meaning to the self and others. Collectivities share meanings, which in turn motivate their members to behave in ways that create economic, political, organizational, familial, and other social structures. So, for instance, Weber argued that capitalism as an economic system arose from a specific world view characteristic of ascetic Protestants (Calvinists), known as the Protestant Ethic.

Weber also responded to Marx's ideas concerning social inequality as embodied in the concept of class. For purposes of this book, the most important part of Weber's discussion of social inequality is his concept of **status**. Social inequality may be a function of economic markets, that is, may be structured around classes. It may also be rooted in symbols, which carry with them status honor or prestige. Aristocratic titles; prestigious family names; the "right" prep school, university, accent, ethnicity, or social club membership; certain types of occupations; or other aspects of consumption and life-style, result in honor for their possessors, even if they lack wealth. Indeed, status honor may help people to accumulate economic advantages (or vice versa). The important point is that, for Weber, social inequality can be a question of differential prestige, in addition to or instead of, differential class.

Analyses of inequality often employ the concept **power**, and in so doing, often use Weber's definition. He defined it as the ability of an actor or group to get other actors or groups to comply with their requests, even in the face of resistance by the others. Often, however, power is legitimated, and thus becomes **authority**. Legitimacy refers to agreement among both the power wielders and compliers that the former have the right to make requests or demands, and the latter have a moral obligation to comply with them.

No theorists call themselves Weberian-feminists. None bases an entire theory of gender on Weberian ideas. However, several feminist theories incorporate specific pieces of Weber's thought, and those just discussed constitute the main ones employed in the theories to be reviewed.

FREUD

The contemporary feminist movement began by thoroughly criticizing and rejecting Freud's theory of psychosexual development. By the mid 1970s, however, a number of feminist scholars had begun to develop their own versions of neo-Freudian theory. These theorists have maintained many of the original concepts and insights, while replacing those aspects which, as feminists, they found problematic. Feminist versions of Freudian theory derive not merely from Freud, but from a variety of theorists who have expanded and revised Freud's theory since his time. However, in this chapter I will confine my discussion to the basic elements in Freud's own theory.

Freud made four key assumptions about people relevant to the "normal" process and results of psychosexual development: (1) that human motivation is rooted in the unconscious, the major wellspring of which are events and relationships that occur in the first five years of life; (2) that the sexual urge constitutes, from the very beginning of life, the major dynamic that motivates human functioning; (3) that childhood development occurs in a set sequence of stages; and (4) that human beings are innately bisexual and become "normal," "appropriately" gendered heterosexuals contingent upon a specific, developmental sequence, involving the actions and reactions of parents during early childhood. This fourth assumption involves the further belief that normal women and men are and ought to be fundamentally different.

At birth, all infants possess a general, unfocused sexual urge, which Freud called the **libido**. Primary gratification is found in relieving hunger through suckling, which quickly becomes generalized to pleasure-seeking through the use of the mouth even when not hungry. This constitutes the **oral stage** of development. During the second and third years of life, children move into the second, **anal stage** of development, where gratification is focused on control over their bowels. This stage emerges as children are praised and rewarded by their parents for developing such control. By age three to four, the locus of gratification shifts to the genitals, as children discover masturbation. Freud gave this stage the masculine label **phallic**, although he postulated that girls as well as boys experience it. Around age six, children enter the **latency stage**, during which they cease to display their sexuality, which lays dormant for several years. Sexual urges reemerge during puberty, at which time children enter the last, **genital stage** of development. In the normal course of events, at this stage the libido is focused on members of the other sex, and males and females display markedly different personalities.

Until they enter the phallic stage, boys and girls experience the same developmental process. Both have as their initial love object their mother, the primary provider of gratification. Both develop their early identification with her. These first years of life which comprise the oral and anal stages are also called the **pre-oedipal stage**. At age three or four, children enter the **oedipal stage** of psychosexual development, and it is at this point that the processes diverge for the sexes.

Freud first developed his ideas about the oedipal stage for boys. His later attempt to develop a female counterpart for this stage was never very successful, even in Freud's own view. That is probably because it was predicated on the earlier, male model. Feminists today do not so much reject his thinking about male development as they do his derived (and therefore contrived) theory pertaining to females.

Normal Male Development

Since their mothers served as the primary source of gratification during the first two stages, as boys enter the phallic stage they continue to expect the same. Freud argued that during this stage boys develop powerful sexual urges directed towards their mothers. They therefore become jealous of and hostile toward their fathers, who already possess the objects of their desire.

In turn, these feelings arouse intense fears and anxieties among boys. They come to fear punishment from their fathers. More specifically, since the penis has become the central focus of their sexual desire, and that desire is provoking the jealousy and anticipated punishment, phallic-stage boys come to fear that their fathers will castrate them. Freud called this **castration anxiety**. Such anxiety is heightened as boys come to discover that there already exist "castrated" people, namely females. Boys presumably reason that if females could lose their penises, so could they. Freud argues that at this stage boys also come to define females as their inferiors because they lack a penis. Moreover, this definition persists into later life.

Unable to live with castration anxiety, normal boys resolve the oedipal phase by repressing their desire to sexually possess their mothers, a repression aided by the negative responses of both parents to sexual overtures to the mother. They also repress their jealousy and hostility toward their fathers. In the process, they switch their primary identification from their mothers to their fathers. In this way, they come to model the behavior of their fathers, learning both appropriate gender behavior and heterosexuality. Freud argued that another major result for boys of the process of resolving the oedipal complex is that they develop a strong **superego**. The superego refers to the internalized moral values and norms of the community (a conscience), which boys presumably develop through their identification with their fathers after repressing their incestuous desires.

Normal Female Development

Freud postulated that the central dynamic which leads girls to their mature, heterosexual development is **penis envy**. During the phallic stage, girls discover, through a comparison with boys, that they lack a penis. They come to define themselves as castrated and incomplete on this basis, thereby developing a permanent sense of inferiority and jealousy. When they learn that no females, including their mothers, possess a penis, they develop a feeling of contempt for their entire gender. This reaction remains later in life. Contempt for women leads them to reject the mother as primary love object, replacing her with the father. The father is viewed by phallic-stage girls as one who can give them the yearned for penis. Mother is now perceived as a rival for the father's love, just as boys perceive the father as a rival for the mother's love. This is sometimes termed the **Electra complex** for girls.

Unlike boys, girls do not experience castration anxiety, inasmuch as they are already "castrated." Because of this, they do not repress their sexual desire for their fathers as strongly as do boys for their mothers. Girls therefore fail to develop a strong superego; as adults, women lack the sense of social justice and conscience that are the hallmark of civilized men. Instead, girls must deal with their penis envy. Normally, they do this by substituting a wish for a baby, especially a boy baby, for their wish for a penis. For Freud, this wish for a baby creates in females a substantial tendency toward masochism. The substitution of baby for penis requires of girls a change of genital focus from clitoris to vagina (an assertion rendered nonsensical by modern physiological research). The result of this transition, according to Freud, is that female sexuality is transformed from active (clitorally oriented) to passive (vaginally oriented). He also argued that penis envy has long-term consequences for the personality development of females. One of these is the trait of narcissism, or a preoccupation with the self and a strong need to be loved. Vanity is another ostensibly feminine trait, which Freud contended arises as compensation for women's genital inferiority. Finally, a sense of shame is said to characterize women, a sense which develops out of their girlhood attempt to conceal their genital deficiency.

Summary

Feminist critiques of Freud's theory of female psychosexual development, and his description of normalcy in women, are many and varied in their particulars. What they share in common is a rejection of the exceptionally high value Freud imputed to the penis for members of both sexes, and therefore the imputation of female genital inferiority. Rather, feminists argue that to the extent that children of both sexes agree on the superiority of maleness, rather than being a universal response to anatomical differences, it is a response to the social superiority of males, which may be symbolized by the penis. Rejected also by feminists is the catalogue of mostly negative traits said to define the normal woman everywhere and at all times. These include Freud's emphasis on the vagina as the locus of mature female sexual response; the supposed lack of a strong superego; and the masochism, narcissism, vanity, jealousy, and sense of shame imputed to women. In short, Freud's theory is seen as compromised by his male-biased assumptions concerning the natural and normal traits and behaviors of men and women. Such assumptions were rooted in the middle-class, Victorian milieu in which he lived and worked. Yet Freud did not limit his theory to a particular time, place, or social class. While he remained concerned that this explanation of female development might be inadequate, he felt that his theory of psychosexual development was generally applicable to the species. As a result, Freud has been criticized as propounding a theory in which "biology is destiny." In the hands of neo-Freudian feminists, the stages and processes of development described by Freud are revised and placed within the context of a male-dominated sociocultural environment. In this way, what Freud defined as everywhere *normal* for each sex becomes that which is *typical* (and not necessarily desirable) in a given type of family and society.

The theories that comprise the Everyday Life approach share a view of social life and individual behavior as ongoing, active processes by which people define and impute meaning to self, interactive situations, and the behaviors of others. This approach asks how people interpret, understand, and construct the interactions in which they are routinely involved, and how such interpretations then influence self-concepts and behaviors. Social structure is viewed as a definitional property that is constantly being created and re-created in the interactive process by the meanings people attribute to their own and to others' behaviors, and especially to their utterances or speech. The two major sociological theories within the Everyday Life approach which have most influenced feminist theory are Symbolic Interactionism and Ethnomethodology. Unlike Marxian and Freudian theory, these contain little that feminists have had to revise or reject. Rather, feminist scholars have applied them to issues of gender that had been previously ignored.

Symbolic Interactionism: Mead

A major component of the Symbolic Interaction tradition, from its early proponent George Herbert Mead to some contemporary theorists, has been an emphasis on the process by which children develop a concept of self and become functioning members of their social community. The feminist derivations of Symbolic Interactionism which center on childhood will be included in the Socialization sections, while any other use of that theoretical approach will be found in sections on Everyday Life sociology.

The classical statement of the Symbolic Interaction perspective is George Herbert Mead's *Mind, Self and Society* (first published posthumously in 1934). Mead argued that there can be no individual sense of self apart from interaction and communication with others. In turn, society or social structure emerges from ongoing acts of communication between people. Human communication, unlike that of other animals, is self-conscious and takes into account the responses of others. This is possible because humans possess the ability to **take the role of the other**, that is, assume the perspective of those with whom they interact, thereby predicting the responses they are likely to receive. People are thus able to imaginatively rehearse alternative lines of action, suppress those likely to be considered inappropriate by others, and select a course of behavior that facilitates cooperation among actors. It is our supposedly unique ability to manipulate symbols and understand or interpret symbols used by others that stands at the root of our other distinctive interactive abilities. Such symbols are largely embodied in a shared language.

Interactions that are patterned, coordinated, and organized among diverse individuals constitute institutions or social structure (also called society by Mead). Such patterning and coordination of activities depend on individuals' ability to take the role or perspective not only of specific (individual) others, but of the **generalized other** as well. The generalized other refers to community or societal attitudes and expectations. In turn, it is constantly in the process of being constructed, reconstructed, and changed by individuals in the process of symbolic interaction with one another.

Human beings develop these abilities progressively from birth, through interaction with **significant others**, especially family members and peers. In the process, they develop a **self**, namely, an assessment and evaluation of themselves as if they were an object, like any other object external to themselves. The general process by which a self-conception emerges involves the crystallization of all the fleeting images of self that derive from each interaction with significant others.

Very young children cannot, of course, manipulate or understand symbols. They do have a concept of **I**, the self as subject responding to others, having needs and wants. The I reacts to stimuli and represents the impulsive tendencies of the individual. In order to develop a self-concept, children must also develop a notion of **me**, the self as object that others and self evaluate and appraise. The me is the self assessed from the vantage point of both significant and generalized others, and is thus unique to humans, according to Mead.

Mead delineated three stages through which children progress in the development of a stable self-concept. Initially, given very limited language skills, children are involved in the **play stage**. Unable to assume the roles of others in anything but a rudimentary fashion, and then only one or two at a time, children at this stage can do little more than imitate a role performed by another (e.g., mother, police officer). As they mature, they enter the **game stage**, at which point they can play complex games (e.g., baseball; Monopoly) interactively with others who are playing different roles. This is possible because they are able to conceptualize potential responses from others at this stage and modify their behavior on that basis. Two major differences between these stages are the number of players involved and the amount and complexity of the rules. The third and final stage occurs when youngsters become able to take the role of the generalized other. The mature person has internalized the generalized other, and in this way the norms and values of the community have become those of the individual. Progression through these stages depends both on language acquisition and on the responses of significant others to the child's behavior. Taking the role of others and imagining their reactions to self arise out of experience with past reactions to behavior by significant others. Language acquisition arises out of the development of shared meanings through interaction with others.

Contemporary Symbolic Interactionism

At least two rather different contemporary schools of Symbolic Interactionism exist, one associated with Manford Kuhn, the other with Herber

Blumer. Kuhn argues that people acquire a core self-concept during the childhood socialization process which shapes and constrains their definitions of situations. This makes individual adult behavior quite predictable; interaction with others is essentially seen as the release of a preexisting core self. Social structure, while defined as the product or outcome of interaction, is viewed as then taking on a stable, independent existence that is resistant to change. Kuhn's views are closely related to those theories that I will discuss in the section on Socialization approaches. By contrast, Blumer emphasizes the situational nature and indeterminancy of both individual behavior and social organization. People constantly define and redefine the situations in which they find themselves, changing not only their definitions but social structure as well. The emphasis is on the constant process of emergence of social structure. This approach de-emphasizes the concept of core self, replacing it with a focus on the creative, spontaneous elements of human behavior. It is closer to Ethnomethodology, which will be discussed shortly.

Labeling Theory

A contemporary offshoot of Symbolic Interactionism is Labeling theory, which has developed in the area of delinquency and deviance. This theory argues that when an individual is formally labeled by others, especially those in positions of authority, in a stigmatizing way ("delinquent," "criminal," "mentally ill"), the person's future behavior is affected. Using the idea of the self-fulfilling prophecy first developed by Robert Merton (not himself a Symbolic Interactionist), Labeling theory argues that the process of formally labeling a person encourages the individual to "live up to" the expectations conveyed by the label. The person, whose initial behavior may have differed little or not at all from that of many others, goes on to create a career in terms of the stigmatized role to which she/he has been assigned by the label. The emphasis in this theory is placed upon the social reaction to the behavior of an individual, and how that reaction, symbolized by a label, creates a self-concept that further encourages the very behavior that prompted the initial negative reaction. Merton's concept of the self-fulfilling prophecy also alerts us to the fact that positive, socially valued labels and expectations of individuals are likely to induce socially desirable behavior by affecting self-concept; that the labeling process can work both to produce socially stigmatized and socially desired behavior

Dramaturgical Approach

One final, contemporary offshoot of Symbolic Interactionism is Irving Goffman's Dramaturgical approach. Especially in his book *The Presentation of Self in Everyday Life* (first published 1959), Goffman focused on the manner in which people consciously manipulate gestures (e.g., language, appearance) to create for others the impressions, the positive images, they want to. He called this **impression management**. People are seen as virtually always acting to an audience that they wish to impress with a particular definition of who they are. Individuals go to great effort to hide stigmatized or socially unacceptable aspects of their selves and lives. In the process of such acting, they become what they pretend to others to be.

Ethnomethodology

The central issue raised by Ethnomethodology asks how people create, sustain, and change their sense of social reality as something concrete and external to themselves. What are the *methods* people use when they interact that create a shared perception of social order? The focus of attention is on the process of creation rather than any presumed substance of social reality. Ethnomethodologists assume that people work constantly and hard at re-creating the social world in order to achieve a sense that the world is orderly and predictable. They seek to understand the everyday, taken-for-granted, implicit rules people use in interacting with one another that allow them to create such a sense. Such rules are called the **stock of knowledge** of a social group, and individuals judged to be competent group members are those who share and demonstrate that stock of knowledge.

The primary way by which people create shared understandings of the social world is through talk that abides by the implicit rules that comprise the stock of knowledge. Indeed, most social interaction is spent talking. When people talk, according to Ethnomethodologists what they are doing is giving **accounts** — telling stories to one another. In recounting stories to one another, people are not merely describing something; they are actually creating for themselves and listeners that which they are describing, which is what Ethnomethodologists term **reflexivity**. Stated otherwise, only as people talk, relating stories to one another, is social reality constructed, and it is accomplished as a shared understanding. In turn, the social reality that is constructed in this manner is seen by participants as compelling certain types of perceptions and behaviors on their part.

Summary

Feminist theorists use Everyday Life approaches in several ways. Some raise the fundamental Ethnomethodological issue of how a social definition of gender is constructed that entails a taken-for-granted perception that two sexes exist, into only one of which all people fit. Others address the process by which people create, in interactive situations, gendered images of self and partner(s). Another issue concerns how, especially through talk, male-female interactions create gender inequality. Underlying all of these Everyday Life feminist theories is the assumption that gender is a social construction that emerges out of microlevel interactions, and that the primary — or at least a very important — mechanism producing a collective perception of gender is communication.

SOCIALIZATION APPROACHES

Although the general theories collected together as the Socialization approach vary in many ways, those who work within these traditions tend to make several assumptions in common. First, they assume that as children, people learn primarily through the mechanisms of rewards and punishments (direct and vicarious) and identification and modeling to conform to the behavioral expectations of others in their social environment. They, therefore, implicitly assume that socialization agents (e.g., parents, teachers, creators of children's media, and so on) can consciously mold children to conform to their ideals to a substantial degree, if they choose. In this they differ from those who work in the Freudian tradition, which stresses the unconscious and very subtle nature of the developmental process.

Second, they assume that during the process of socialization most individuals develop personal commitments to the norms, values, and behaviors they are learning; that is, they **internalize** their social roles. In this way, that which is socially expected of people becomes, for the most part, that which people define as good and proper and expect of themselves. Finally, they assume that a core identity is developed through the childhood socialization process, which is, with only some modification, usually the basis of a rather consistent, lifelong, self-concept. Thus, the behaviors and attitudes of adults are viewed largely as reflections of early childhood learning, and in any given situation peoples' actions are seen as relatively straightforward reflections of their core selves. In this they are similar to some aspects of Symbolic Interactionism.

Besides that aspect of Symbolic Interactionism dealing with childhood socialization which was already reviewed, the two socialization theories that have had the most influence on feminist sociologists come from psychology: Social Learning and Cognitive Development. I will begin this section with a discussion of the concept status/role and basic elements of Role theory, since social roles involve both socialization and structural dimensions. I will then move to the two psychological theories. As in the case of Everyday Life approaches, with the exception of Lawrence Kohlberg's theory of moral development, feminist theorists have found little to reject in the Socialization approaches. Rather, their efforts have been directed to applying general theoretical insights to specific issues concerning the development and effects of gender differences, issues left underdeveloped by earlier theorists.

Role Theory

Many Socialization theories, as well as much of Symbolic Interactionist theory, implicitly if not explicitly assume the existence of **status/roles**. A social role is a set of expectations concerning the appropriate behavior of people who are incumbents of a position or status (e.g., student, physician, father). Role theorists define the status/role as the basic element of structure. They assume that, except during periods of rapid role change, role definitions are typically widely agreed upon by societal members; that is, that there is general consensus concerning the expectations of appropriate behavior for incumbents of a given status. Those expectations are viewed as comprising a **script** that leaves some room for individual variation, innovation, and negotiation, but nonetheless establishes specific **norms** (rules) of behavior when interacting with people playing complementary roles. Many status/roles are **achieved** on the basis of some action or effort (e.g., student, any employment role). Others are **ascribed** on the basis of an inherent characteristic that individuals cannot alter (e.g., age statuses such as infant or senior citizen). Differential rewards, such as prestige, money, and power, attach to various statuses, both achieved and ascribed. Therefore, another fundamental component of social structure is the rank order of statuses, or the stratification system.

At any given time in their lives, individuals play a variety of roles because they occupy a number of statuses. Specific types of status/roles often tend to cluster together (e.g., corporate executive/husband/father/community leader). Some roles articulate well with others (e.g., husband and employee), while others involve expectations that will probably conflict with some frequency if held by the same person (e.g., mother and army officer). Status/roles with a higher probability of producing conflicting obligations are less likely to cluster than those which are not likely to do so. Since individuals occupy a variety of statuses at any one time in life, and are therefore subject to numerous role obligations and expectations, some types of status/role usually assume priority over others. Under conditions of role conflict or strain, those status/roles that have lower priority to the individual are often reduced or sacrificed. The rank order of role priority is, in substantial measure, socially not individually defined.

Many feminist sociologists have conceptualized gender as ascribed status/roles, which entail relatively detailed scripts concerning appropriate masculine and feminine behavior. Virtually all feminist Socialization and some feminist Symbolic Interactionist theories explore the process by which girls and boys learn and internalize their appropriate gender roles. Other feminist theories have focused on adults, examining the relationships between ascribed gender roles assumed to have been learned during childhood and the probability of achieving other social roles, especially highly valued and rewarded ones. Among other things, they examine the ways in which gender roles affect the priority of other status/roles for individuals and how gender roles influence the choices people make concerning which specific types of achieved status/roles to pursue. Feminist applications of Role theory which do not deal with childhood socialization may be found in other sections of the book. Their placement will vary according to the particular focus of the theory.

Social Learning Theory

Social Learning theory asserts that humans learn through two processes: direct and vicarious experience. Direct learning occurs in response to rewards (reinforcements) and punishments received in reaction to behavior. But people don't have to directly experience something in order to learn; we can learn vicariously by observing the responses (rewarding or punishing) others receive for their behavior. For behavior to be learned through observation of others, the learner must first pay attention to a person who serves as a **model**. Individuals are most inclined to model another person to whom they have a close emotional attachment. Specific behaviors are more likely to be imitated when they anticipate that imitating the model's behavior will be rewarding in itself or rewarded by others. If, however, the model's behavior elicits punishment for the model, the learner is likely to inhibit similar behavior. Social Learning theorists also point out that people may learn behaviors yet not perform them. Thus, for instance, observing a punitive response to a model's behavior may inhibit the performance of that behavior, which may nonetheless have been learned. That behavior is therefore latent and potentially available for performance, if conditions change to make it less likely to elicit punishment or even likely to be rewarded.

Although this process may be sufficient to describe early childhood learning, it is clear that after that point people do not simply respond in each situation by calculating rewards and punishments. Rather, they become self-regulating by internally rewarding themselves with feelings of pride and satisfaction (or by punishing themselves with feelings of guilt and mortification) in response to their own behavior. In short, early learning teaches behavior that is approved by others, which standards are then internalized so that later conformity to them produces an internal reward.

For feminist theorists, the primary issue that arises from Social Learning theory concerns the kinds of behavior that are rewarded and punished on the basis of the gender of the children and the models who exhibit them.

Cognitive Development Theory

Cognitive Development theory is traced to the Swiss psychologist Jean Piaget. He proposed that children must pass through a series of four stages of mental development as they mature. The first year and a half of life comprises the **sensorimotor stage** and comprehension is in terms of the physical characteristics of objects. Stage two lasts until age seven and is termed **preoperational**. Children become adept at manipulating symbols but their perception focuses only on the most salient, obvious features of an object. From ages seven to eleven children are in the **concrete-operational stage**, where they begin to be able to comprehend abstract qualities such as relational terms. The final, mature stage is termed **formal operations**, and at this point individuals are fully capable of abstract and systematic reasoning. From this perspective, children are incapable of learning various things until they reach the stage required for that type of learning. Therefore, young children understand the world in ways that are fundamentally different from that of adults, although this is often not obvious. Nonetheless, Piaget stressed that the developmental process is scarcely a passive, biologically determined unfolding of potentials. Children actively seek out experiences that expedite their cognitive development, and parents, schools, peers, and so on, behave in ways that facilitate or hinder it.

Piaget also claimed that children's moral development goes through parallel stages, an idea most fully developed by the contemporary psychologist Lawrence Kohlberg. Kohlberg has developed a six-stage model of moral development, beginning with **preconventional morality**, when children believe that obedience to authority is inherently right but also fear punishment for rule breaking. Skipping to adolescence, **conventional morality** emerges, based on the belief that the existing social order is good and that proper behavior will make others consider the individual a good person. Only some people reach the highest level of adult moral development, **postconventional morality**. At this stage the relativity of rules is recognized and morality is defined in terms of abstract, fundamental ethical principles. How far and fast individuals progress in their moral development is a function of their sociocultural environment.

Kohlberg's rank order of levels of moral development has been criticized by feminist theorists, especially Carol Gilligan in her book *In A Different Voice* (1982). She accused it of serious masculine bias. The bias occurs in ranking abstract moral reasoning (stage 6) considerably higher than moral reasoning based on personal relationships and obligations (about stage 3). She argued that the latter is more characteristic of adult female morality and the former of adult male morality, but that a morality based on personal relationships is not in fact inferior to one based on abstract principles.

Several feminist theorists use elements of Cognitive Development theory, primarily in conjunction with other Socialization approaches, in an attempt to understand the process by which gender differentiation is created in childhood.

SOCIAL EXCHANGE THEORY

Social Exchange theories typically posit that all human relationships—direct and indirect—are based on a more or less conscious exchange of **rewards** between actors. In social life, these rewards are rarely monetary. Rather, they consist of such things as social approval, esteem, affection or love, and very importantly, compliance to requests. In all relationships actors also incur **costs**, such as giving compliance or forgoing the opportunity for other possible relationships or activities. Furthermore, actors bring to relationships a variety of **investments** — personal characteristics, talents, skills — that are evaluated as more or less valuable by the partners to the relationship. In most cases, relationships continue to the extent that the actors involved receive a **profit**; that is, the rewards exceed the total of costs plus investments.

Homans and Blau

Upon this simple scaffold, several more subtle elements have been added. The first of these are George Homans's concept of **distributive justice** and Peter Blau's of **fair exchange**, which are similar to one another. These concepts arise from recognition of the fact that, unlike economic exchanges, in social exchanges there is no clear way to establish how much of one kind of reward is equal to how much of another kind (e.g., how much compliance compensates for long hours of listening to a friend's troubles?). For Homans, the issue of distributive justice is one of an actor considering whether the amount of profit is enough, given her/his costs and investments. If it isn't, despite the presence of some level of profit, the actor is likely to react with anger. For Blau, the issue is essentially one of equity of profit, which, he argues, is resolved in long-term relationships through the creation by the partners of norms defining fair exchange. He too pointed to a negative reaction by an actor to violations of fair exchange by the partner.

Both theorists also developed a **principle of satiation**. When the same type of reward is received frequently, it becomes less valuable to the recipient. Therefore, that reward will not have the same motivational effect on her/his behavior toward the exchange partner. Borrowing from anthropology, Blau further posited that in stable relationships, a **norm of reciprocity** arises. Rewards proffered by one actor entail reciprocal obligations by the other, which then guide future interactions between them (e.g., you listened to my troubles when I got divorced; I owe you the same attention when, in the future, the need arises). Blau also offered the insight that social life is a series of dilemmas: as people invest in one exchange relationship, they are apt to slight one or more other relationships. Therefore, as one becomes more stabilized and balanced, others become more unstabilized and unbalanced. Because of this, and because inevitably fair exchange and the norm of reciprocity will be violated, conflict is inherent in all long-term relationships.

Blau (unlike Homans) introduced the concept of power into his Exchange theory. He argued that compliance is the most valued type of reward in social exchanges. People are able to extract compliance from their partners when they can withhold resources needed by, or very important to, the other and for which no substitute source is available, or when the other has insufficient resources to meet the norm of fair exchange. This capacity is defined as power. To the extent that the person with power provides valued resources, the partner is likely to accept subordination and legitimate the authority of the powerful partner. However, if the empowered actor violates the norms of reciprocity or fair exchange, or otherwise imbalances the relationship, then the subordinate is likely to withdraw legitimacy and enter into conflict with her/his superior. These principles apply both to direct, interpersonal (microlevel) relationships, and at the macrolevel where the social exchange is often indirect.

Thibaut and Kelley

One final set of concepts important to Social Exchange theory was developed by psychologists John Thibaut and Harold Kelley: **Comparison Level** and **Comparison Level of Alternatives**. Over time and the experience of many social exchanges, people develop a standard against which to weigh and assess their relative satisfaction with the outcome of a particular exchange relationship. This standard constitutes the Comparison Level. When involved in a given relationship, actors compare their satisfaction (profits) to that standard, but also to their perceptions of the likely or feasible alternatives—the Comparison Level of Alternatives. If the latter appears worse than the existing relationship, regardless of how unsatisfactory it may be (how negative the profit), the actor will continue in it.

Summary

Feminist sociologists have not been critical of Social Exchange theory. Rather, a few have applied it to gender relationships, particularly familial relationships. It has probably received less attention from feminists than its potential warrants, although the basic theory itself is fraught with logical problems that have been well explored in the general sociological theory literature.

CONCLUSION

The preceding sections exemplify the substantial diversity of theoretical perspectives upon which feminist theorists have drawn. In the next four chapters I will review a large number of specific feminist theories, many of which are explicit versions of one of the theoretical traditions reviewed in this chapter. Other feminist theories incorporate insights from one or more of these traditions, and some are not directly related to any of them. I begin in the next chapter with feminist theories that attempt to explain the origins or fundamental causes of gender inequality.

2 CAUSES OF GENDER INEQUALITY

Everywhere one looks—now and historically—there are indications that the sexes are unequal. In most modern societies, employed women average between half and three-quarters the income of employed men. Few women have ever occupied high-level positions in government or in large economic organizations in any society. When employed, women virtually everywhere enjoy less leisure than their husbands, because they remain responsible for most unpaid domestic work. In many parts of the world, women routinely receive less food, and when infanticide is practiced, it is largely female babies that die. Family decision making is typically dominated by men, who are usually defined as head-of-household. In most cultures and many religions, males and masculinity are defined as more worthy than females and femininity. The specifics vary from one society or time to another, but women are, and probably have always been at least somewhat disadvantaged relative to men in their society. Why? In this chapter different theoretical perspectives that attempt to explain the causes or origins of systems of gender inequality are examined.

Some feminist theories, especially those developed before the mid 1970s, assumed that women everywhere and at all times have been substantially disadvantaged or oppressed relative to men in their societies. In the absence of that assumption, there was sometimes a tendency to simply dichotomize the world into cases of sexual equality and those of female oppression. However, anthropological literature that accumulated during the early 1970s demonstrated that societies have varied along a continuum from minimal gender inequality to extreme female disadvantage. More recent theoretical work thus often looks at the determinants of variation in gender inequality, rather than being couched in terms of the causes of female oppression.

The variable of concern in this chapter is called by some the **gender** (sex) **stratification system**. Other terms relating to gender inequality include male dominance, sexism, female oppression, and patriarchy. Such terminological differences are often related to other theoretical differences. In this book the various terms will be considered as synonyms for one another, and I will not be concerned with fine points of difference between them.

The topics for this and the next chapter — the causes of gender inequality and mechanisms that maintain and reproduce such systems — appear to be distinctly different. Indeed, logically they are. A given variable may be of fundamental importance in causing something to come into existence, yet once a system exists may be of little or no importance in its maintenance. Conversely, mechanisms may develop once a system exists which function as strong bulwarks of that system, yet played no part in causing the emergence of the phenomenon in question. Theories of gender do not always clearly distinguish between these two types of variables and analyses. This failure typically works in one direction: that apparently causal theories are in fact theories of maintenance or reproduction. In this case, a theoretical assertion ostensibly dealing with cause implicitly and unwittingly assumes preexisting gender inequality (see Cucchiari, 1981:40-1). I have tried to sort theories into the two chapters according to my judgement about such assumptions. Moreover, in some instances I explicitly point out that a particular theory is indeed one of maintenance, despite the author's assertion that it is causal; or at least that a major causal factor is missing from the argument, and the theory therefore begins by assuming the very inequality it purports to explain. It is, however, impossible to draw a line distinguishing causal from maintenance theories with total precision.

The theories explored in this chapter are, with a few exceptions, macrostructural. In general, microinteractionist theories are much better suited to explaining how gender systems are reproduced and maintained than what causes them in the first place. Therefore, most of the microperspectives will not be introduced until the next chapter.

MARXIST-FEMINIST EXPLANATIONS

A vast Marxist-feminist literature has emerged since the late 1960s, written by scholars from different humanistic and social scientific disciplines. I have chosen a few, mostly recent works, which I think adequately express the range of Marxist-feminist issues and concepts. In general, Marxist-feminists tend to stress the concrete, historically specific aspects of systems of oppression. While they clearly develop and employ abstract concepts and general theoretical principles, most explicitly reject an attempt to generalize beyond a given type of socioeconomic system. I have concentrated on those who do in fact generalize, in order not to become bogged down in detailed analyses of specific historical cases. (I consider such analyses to represent the application of theory rather than its development, although the line between the two is blurry.)

SACKS

A general analysis of the causes of female oppression is that of anthropologist Karen Sacks, who revised Engels's theory of female subordination in light of modern anthropological data (1974). She began by reinterpreting two basic concepts employed by Engels, **social labor** and **production for exchange**. Sacks defined social labor "to include any work done (singly or as part of a group) for use or appropriation by someone of another household." This is juxtaposed to **domestic work**, or that done only for one's own household. Production for exchange potentially involves two fundamentally different phenomena. Sacks argued that in all societies people give gifts, which obligate the recipient to make a return. If everyone is equal in their access to the means of subsistence, everyone is capable of making an equal return. However, when the means of subsistence are privately, hence unequally held, the recipient cannot return a gift of equal worth. Rather, the recipient is expected to return the favor with service. This gives the property owner the "ability to harness the labor power of others for his own ends." It is this second situation that Sacks called **production for exchange**, referring to the first as **production for use** (1974:212).

Sacks's main thesis is that women's status is a function of social labor, for it is such labor that makes people **social adults**. With the simultaneous development of private property, production for exchange, and class society, however, women's labor becomes domestic and they cease to be social adults. Even in nonclass societies lacking private property, men and women are not completely equal. Sacks argued that women may simultaneously be social adults and "wifely wards": that women's status within marriage seems to vary independently of their status in the larger society (1974:211). Their marital status, in turn, is a function of which spouse owns the household property. However, if women are regarded as social adults, the extent to which they may be subordinated within the household is limited. Conversely, wifely subservience reduces the ability of women to exercise their social adulthood (1974:218).

Examining class societies more closely, Sacks noted that property ownership per se does not constitute the basis for male supremacy because many
men do not own productive property and because individual women often
do. When women do own property, they may have substantial domestic
power, but that will not translate into social power in the public sphere
(1974:219). If property ownership doesn't explain female social subordination in class societies, what does? Sacks argued that it is their exclusion from
social labor, hence social adulthood: "It seems that class societies tend to socialize the work of men and to domesticate that of women." By denying social adulthood to women, the ruling class comes to define them as wards of
men. The next issue, then, is why this happens, and Sacks claimed:

> Ruling classes select men as social laborers partly because they are
> more mobile, but probably more significantly because they can be
> more intensively exploited than women, not having to nurse and
> rear children. (1974:220)

This division of labor results in the relegation of women "to the bottom
of a social pecking order." Moreover, the necessary and important function
of rearing future generations of exchange workers is forced upon women
without compensation. Under modern capitalism, women have become
more involved in social labor, but domestic labor remains their responsibility. Continued domestic responsibility, in turn, creates barriers to women's
social labor and places them in a more exploitable position than men in the
labor force (1974:221). In short, men were originally preferred for social labor within class societies because their labor was more exploitable. Once
women came to be defined as inadequate for public labor, the conditions
were right for capitalism to discover them as a source of cheap labor. In both
instances, the ruling class has profited. Sacks further argued that the ruling
class has compensated men for their loss of work autonomy with the subordination of women and the household to men and the larger society,
legitimating this through an ideology of differential worth (1974:222).

EISENSTEIN

Zillah Eisenstein is a Marxist-feminist political scientist who has attempted
to integrate the Marxian emphasis on economic exploitation with the radical
feminist concentration on patriarchy, as rooted in women's reproductive
functions (1979). With special focus on capitalist systems, she asserted that
patriarchy and capitalism are analytically distinct forms of oppression which
are concretely intertwined and mutually supportive in any given case. Patriarchy predates capitalism, she argued. However, the particular form taken by
patriarchy in a capitalist system is a function both of historical continuity and
of changes resulting from its interconnections with capitalist relations of

production. In addition, Eisenstein claimed that because they are distinct (albeit interrelated) forms of oppression, the abolition of one does not automatically result in the abolition of the other, as has been apparent in socialist societies (1979:24).

Women's oppression within capitalist societies is a result both of their economic exploitation as wage laborers, and their patriarchal oppression as mothers, domestic laborers, and consumers (1979:22). This oppression has both a material and an ideological dimension, two factors that are tightly interwoven (1979:24). The ideology of patriarchy is rooted in social interpretations of biological (reproductive) differences between the sexes. The concrete, institutional form this takes is the sexual division of labor and the nuclear family. In short, where economic exploitation is rooted in the relations of production, patriarchal oppression is rooted in the relations of reproduction (1979:25). Both types of oppression find expression in the family and in the economy.

Patriarchal relations are malleable to the needs of capitalism, and vice versa (1979:27). For instance, Eisenstein argued that capitalists' need for cheap labor, which women supply, has not resulted in the full integration of women into all parts of the labor force, out of deference to patriarchy's need to protect male superiority. The result is job segregation. Thus, "the sexual definition of women as mother [i.e., the ideology of patriarchy] either keeps her in the home doing unpaid labor or enables her to be hired at a lower wage because of her defined sexual inferiority" (1979:29). In turn, patriarchy serves the needs of capitalism because the sexual division of labor stabilizes the society through the family, while it organizes domestic labor at no pay or limited pay. In this way, the capitalists profit, along with all men regardless of class, from women's oppression (1979:30–1).

In a comparison with precapitalist modes of production, Eisenstein argued that women's oppression under capitalism has become increasingly institutionalized as women's place became specifically defined in terms of the nuclear family (1979:30). She located the reason for this in the removal of men from home-based production alongside women into the wage-labor economy. Left behind at home, women were increasingly viewed by men as nonproductive. Productive labor came to be defined as wage labor, that is, labor that produces surplus value. Before capitalism women were mothers, but this was not an exclusive role. With capitalism women became housewives (1979:30). Even when functioning within the capitalist economy, the segregated types of work women perform make them serve as domestic laborer and nurturer of the social world, because of patriarchal ideology. In addition, women assume a role necessary to capitalism as consumer who both buys and cares for goods (1979:48).

While very briefly positing a possible initial cause for patriarchy, Eisenstein makes it clear that gender hierarchy in contemporary societies reflects not conditions at the point of origin, but those that have evolved historically into contemporary ones (1979:49). Thus, to understand women's oppression today one must understand both that historical evolution of patriarchy and its interconnectedness with modern capitalism. In short, the cause of gender inequality is not universal but specific to concrete systems at given periods of time.

VOGEL

In a similar manner, Lise Vogel began her analysis by carefully noting that a full understanding of women's oppression must always come from an analysis of the specific history of any given society, and that it is unproductive to search for some ultimate theoretical cause of it (1983:148). Nonetheless, she developed an abstract theory that situates the phenomenon of women's oppression in terms of social reproduction within class societies (1983:137), and then showed how these dynamics function in specifically capitalist ones.

All modes of production simultaneously entail two aspects: the process of producing something (a specific product) and the process of reproducing the mode of production itself (1983:138). Reproduction entails two things: sustaining the conditions of productive labor, that is, reproducing the operating conditions; and maintaining and reproducing laborers. Reproduction and production are not the same, and the former is not an aspect or form of the latter. Likewise, maintenance of laborers and replacement of the labor force are not the same phenomena, and neither is a form of the other. In most societies, both of the reproduction functions are fulfilled within the family, although neither must be (1983:141). For Vogel, the reproduction of labor power refers specifically to the maintenance and renewal of the exploited class of workers. The ruling class must also be maintained and renewed, but this is a separate issue.

In the process of their labor, workers engage in necessary labor and surplus labor. **Necessary labor** refers to that part of their total labor time required to achieve their own reproduction. **Surplus labor** is the residual labor time that ruling class members exploit for their own profit. It is in the interests of the ruling class to minimize necessary labor time, thereby increasing surplus labor time. In turn, necessary labor is comprised of three parts: maintenance of the producers (workers); maintenance of nonlaboring members of the working class; and generational replacement (i.e., bearing and rearing workers' children).

Until this point in Vogel's analysis, there is nothing that is gender-specific. The one fundamental difference between men and women is that generational replacement must be done by women. This fact lies at the root of women's oppression in class society (1983:145). Childbearing and lactation serve in the short run to diminish women's contributions as producers of both surplus and necessary labor. Their value to the ruling class is thereby reduced. However, the longer-term interests of the ruling class require that the labor force be replenished through generational replacement. There is thus an inherent contradiction between the long- and short-run interests of the ruling class in terms of women's reproductive capacity. This contradiction has usually been resolved by taking advantage of those preexisting sexual and kinship arrangements called the family, making males responsible for providing sustenance to childbearing women. While in principle such arrangements could be confined to a few months, in reality they are not, and men and women are assigned different familial roles. Women become primarily responsible for necessary labor, including childcare, men for the provision of the material means of subsistence (wages), which is accompanied by a greater involvement in surplus labor (1983:146). The result, stated Vogel, is as follows:

> The exact form by which men obtain more means of subsistence than needed for their own individual consumption varies from society to society, but the arrangement is ordinarily legitimated by their domination of women and reinforced by institutionalized structures of female oppression. The ruling class, in order to stabilize the reproduction of labor power as well as to keep the amount of necessary labor at acceptable levels, encourages male supremacy within the exploited class. (1983:147)

Thus, argued Vogel, it is men's providing the means of subsistence to women, not the sexual division of labor per se, that stands at the root of women's subordination in class systems. Such subordination is lessened, however, where the importance of generational replacement of the labor force is minimized, such as where migrant workers constitute the working class or when capitalists place their emphasis on the immediate production of surplus value and ignore the reproduction of the labor force (1983:149–50).

This analysis has concerned the exploited class. But women in the ruling class are also subordinate to men of their own class. Like working class women, their subordination rests on their role in generational replacement. For members of the ruling class, the bequeathment of property to children brings about female oppression as a mechanism to ensure the paternity of those children (1983:148).

In general, these processes are exacerbated under capitalism. Necessary labor becomes bifurcated into: (1) a social component, which is totally bound up with surplus labor, and consists of that portion of labor time for which the worker is paid wages necessary for sustenance; and (2) a domestic component, or that part of necessary labor performed outside of the sphere of capitalist production, which turns workers' wages into directly consumable goods. This goes hand in hand with a severe separation between those sites and social units where social and surplus labor are performed and those where domestic labor is performed (1983:153). Needless to add, social and surplus labor become men's province, domestic labor women's. This, in turn, strengthens the historical legacy of female subordination inherited from an earlier class system. Moreover, this strong demarcation between domestic and wage labor "forms the basis for a series of powerful ideological structures, which develop a forceful life of their own." The separation of men's and women's work and worlds comes to be defined as natural in an ideology of separate spheres (1983:154).

Since capitalists seek to increase surplus value, they attempt to reduce necessary labor time, including domestic labor. According to Vogel, capitalists accomplish this by partially socializing domestic tasks through the creation of such profit-making services as fast-food chains, laundromats, and stores selling ready-made clothing, and also by supporting public services such as schools. This, in turn, frees up more of women's time to engage in surplus, that is wage, labor. However, it is too expensive and unprofitable to totally socialize necessary labor in capitalist societies. That which remains unsocialized remains disproportionately performed by women, and is accompanied by a system of male supremacy (1983:154–6, 170).

Vogel argued that the economic basis of women's oppression within capitalism that I have just reviewed is supplemented by a lack of full democratic rights for women. Since its inception, capitalism has sought to create formal equality of persons, in order to maximize workers' freedom to sell their labor on an open market (1983:162–5). This has entailed the gradual extension of democratic rights to various segments of the society. Women's lack of formal equality, or full democratic rights, unlike that of any other social group, has been a function of their capacity to bear children. Therefore, "obstacles to the achievement of real social equality for women have their own character, separable from those blocking equality for other groups" (1983:166). This affects all women, regardless of social class. In turn, this has permitted discrimination against women as they increasingly engage in surplus production (wage labor) (1983:168).

In summary, Vogel argued that women's oppression is rooted in the fact that, because of their reproductive functions, women come to perform necessary labor within the domestic unit. In turn, this limits their ability to engage in social labor, including the production of surplus value. Both forms of labor are required for a class system to persist. This economic factor is coupled with a unique form of sociopolitical inequality in capitalistic systems. In turn, this permits continued gender inequality, even as women's domestic labor is reduced and their involvement in social labor increases. The concrete workings of these abstract processes vary considerably from one context to another. However, Vogel concluded that there can never be gender equality within a capitalist system.

WARD

In her book *Women in the World-System* (1984), Kathryn Ward has extended Marxian-based World Systems theory by explicating how and why the process of economic development is reducing the relative status of women in dependent (peripheral) nations. She summarized her work as demonstrating that, in such nations, "the intrusion of the world-system through foreign investment from and trade dependency on core nations has operated to reduce women's status relative to men's" (1984:3). She was not proposing a general theory of gender stratification. Rather, she offered an explanation of why it is increasing in a particular kind and large number of societies in the contemporary world.

Ward argued that the World Systems perspective has omitted a crucial variable from its analyses, which she termed **patriarchal relations**. She defined this

> as the institutionalized patterns and ideologies of male dominance and control over resources that have generally empowered men to define the productive roles and behavior of women. (1984:14–15)

It is comprised of both the actual mechanisms by which men control existing resources and the sexual division of labor, and the ideologies which justify the resulting sexual inequality. The exportation of Western (core nation) capitalism and ideology to peripheral nations has generally served to strengthen patriarchal relations in the latter societies. The relative economic demand for women's work or motherhood roles, as defined by the contingencies of capitalism and patriarchal relations, determines the economic status of women (1984:19). In other words, women's status in peripheral nations is a function of the local effects of capitalist decision making emanating from core countries, combined with the strengthened position of males (patriarchal relations) in their own societies.

How, in more precise terms, does the world expansion of capitalism reduce women's status? Ward pointed to a number of mechanisms. Preexisting patriarchal relations and Western bias support a system in which indigenous males in peripheral societies are typically given control over the economic resources and superior access to the economic opportunities introduced by foreign firms. The result of greater male access to, and control over, the monetarized and industrial sectors of the economy is a new sexual division of labor (1984:21). Likewise, newly developing political and educational institutions have been placed primarily in the hands of men. Women have been largely confined to the precapitalist economy of subsistence agriculture and small-scale handicrafts and trade, which suffer extensively from the introduction of factory-produced goods, large-scale commerce, and foreign trade, all in the hands of men. Women in some nations do gain access to new factory positions on the **global assembly line**. These are jobs that have been exported from core nations (e.g., textile and electronics assembly), but the pay is poor (barely subsistence level), the jobs are insecure, and only unmarried women are employed. Moreover, those young women who do work on them are closely controlled by a patriarchal management. Other opportunities are confined to service employment—especially domestic service. In short, women's economic opportunities are generally restricted to subsistence agriculture, the informal economy of petty trade, service, and handicrafts, or the exploited global assembly line, while men's opportunities are typically expanding in the more modernized sectors of the society.

Ward argued that the extent to which women suffer from reduced opportunities, relative to men in their society, is primarily a function of the extent of the peripheral nation's trade dependency on core nations and the level of foreign investment: the greater the dependency and investment levels, the greater the gender inequality. A series of intervening variables are posited as linking economic dependency and foreign investment to the status of women. These include governmental policies concerning women, the strength of indigenous women's organizations, the degree to which women are unionized, the overall level of income inequality, women's relative educational resources, the level of population growth relative to labor force growth, the level of urbanization, the relative size of the tertiary (service) sector of the economy, and of course the strength of patriarchal relations (1984:40–43).

BENNHOLDT-THOMSEN

Veronika Bennholdt-Thomsen is a more explicit Marxist-feminist working within the World Systems approach. The thrust of her theoretical essay (1984) was to demonstrate that the socioeconomic category of housewife is relatively new; it emerged, together with the category of wage worker, during the rise of the capitalist world system (1984:253). Moreover, it has spread in recent years to encompass even the peasantry of Third World nations (1984:263). Implicit in this discussion is the idea that in the contemporary world, the housewife status ascribed to all women on the castelike basis of sex is the root cause of gender inequality.

Bennholdt-Thomsen argued that in precapitalist societies, while work was divided along sex lines, both sexes were involved in subsistence labor. Therefore, the sexual division of labor was part of the social division of labor. With capitalism comes a sharp split between commodity and subsistence production and the assignment of the latter almost exclusively to women on the basis of ascription: the social division of labor becomes a sexual one

(1984:267). As capitalism has penetrated nations across the globe, so too has this transformation. In turn, an image of womanhood develops under capitalism that attributes the qualities deemed necessary to housewifery to women on the basis of their supposed nature as females (1984:253). Therefore, even when engaged in commodity production, the kinds of work they are involved in are established on the basis of sex, on an image of women defined in terms of the housewife. Men's work is not, however, defined by sex (1984:254).

Given this division of labor, men and women in capitalist societies are more intimately linked because they need each other. Nonetheless, the sexes are also much more distant from each other than ever before. Social hierarchy is based on occupations and is thus male hierarchy; women do not have a ranking of their own (1984:264). The result is that

> Men form society, women are non-society; men are the true human beings, women are "not human beings"; . . . male labor is socially visible, female labor is invisible. All this is due to the transformation of subsistence production from being social production in earlier periods to being private nowadays, to its exclusive ascription to women, and to the assignment of one, single female producer to one man. (1984:264–5)

She concluded, in a manner more extreme than most Marxist-feminists, that "the sexual division of labor, which is based on the housewife, is not truly an historical remnant. . . . It genuinely belongs to our capitalist mode of production" (1984:266). Therefore, gender inequality under capitalism may be considered to rest on its own unique foundation.

Summary

Taken together, how do these various Marxist-feminist theories constitute a unified perspective applicable to the explanation of the causes of gender inequality? Marxist-feminism recognizes that patriarchy predates capitalism. It is seen as rooted in the institution of the family. In various ways, theorists in this tradition suggest that women's childbearing and lactating functions affect the division of labor between the sexes, leaving women a preponderance of the domestic and childrearing tasks, regardless of what other labor they perform. Therefore, the roots of gender inequality are to be found in a sexual division of labor in which males provide much or all of the family subsistence. This division of labor is posited to arise with the dawning of private property and to be seriously exacerbated by the particular system of private property known as capitalism. Marxist-feminists usually devote the bulk of their attention to exploring the many ways by which capitalism and patriarchy affect and support one another, in effect constituting a unique system of female oppression. In very general terms, that system is marked by virtually total separation of domestic and childrearing tasks from productive labor, with the former assigned to women who thereby become totally dependent on their wage-earning husbands. Such a division of labor is seen as profitable for capitalists in several different ways. Because of this, and especially in return for men's willingness to work as wage laborers, capitalism develops economic policies (e.g., lower wages for women; jobs segregated by sex), governmental policies, and an ideology supportive of patriarchy. Therefore, even when women enter the labor force, they remain oppressed, both by low wages and limited opportunities and by continued responsibility for domestic and childrearing labor. Moreover, as the influence of capitalism spreads worldwide, the oppression of women deepens and takes on new dimensions in heretofore noncapitalist societies.

ANTHROPOLOGICAL APPROACHES

Like sociology, anthropology contains a variety of theoretical perspectives. When feminist anthropologists use a specific theoretical tradition discussed in this book, I include that work with others from that tradition, as in the last section where Karen Sacks's Marxist-feminist theory was discussed. In this section, all other types of feminist anthropological theories will be collected together. They are set apart from the eclectic structural theories developed by sociologists, to be discussed in the next section, for two reasons. First, several of the sociological theories are indebted to theories reviewed in this section. Second, by and large the theories in this section pertain to technologically simple, preliterate societies. Sociological theories are usually oriented to technologically sophisticated, more complex societies. Despite these considerations, the theories in the two sections are in fact closely related.

SANDAY

A major emphasis in the general anthropological tradition has been upon the central importance of cultural definitions and belief systems in shaping social structure. In her book *Female Power and Male Dominance* (1981), Peggy Sanday developed a theory of the causes of male dominance based on a study of a large number of technologically simple, tribal societies, which reflects this concern with cultural phenomena. In addition, it also emanates from a sociological tradition, dating back to such nineteenth century sociologists as Emile Durkheim and Max Weber, which stresses the central importance of a society's religious thought system in shaping social relations and institutions. To some extent, it can be said that Sanday's approach reflects philosophical idealism, the opposite of Marxian materialism.

Each culture has its own **sex-role plan**. Such plans manifest extensive diversity cross-culturally (Sanday, 1981:especially chapters 1-2). This plan specifies how relationships between the sexes are to be structured: "The sexes are either merged or they are segregated; the power to make decisions is either vested in both sexes or is dominated by one sex" (1981:15). In turn, sex-role plans are rooted in a general, overarching cultural orientation. Sanday divided such orientations into two types, inner and outer, depending on the societal definition and perception of nature. An **inner orientation** characterizes societies

> where the forces of nature are sacralized, . . . there is a reciprocal flow between the power of nature and the power inherent in women. The control and manifestation of these forces is left to women and to sacred natural symbols. . . . (1981:5)

An inner orientation places strong emphasis on the female creative principle (1981:33), rooted in maternity. In an **outer orientation**, power is outside of humans; nature is perceived as an uncontrollable force that may strike at any time and against which people must be prepared to defend themselves. It is an orientation based on fear, conflict, and strife (1981:35). This is seen by Sanday as a basically masculine orientation, rooted in men's activities as hunters and warriors (1981:5).

The general orientation of a culture is embodied in its **creation myths**, in which a people make a basic statement about their relationship with nature and about their perception of the source of power in the universe (1981:57). Such myths may include both or only one sex. When only males are involved as mythical agents of creation, there exists an outer orientation and a sex-role plan that makes males dominant. Where females are involved, either alone or as part of a couple, the sex-role plan will reflect, in part or entirely, an inner orientation. It will be more equalitarian.

If variation in the extent of male dominance is explained as the result of different sex-role plans, which, in turn, are rooted in general cultural orientations as reflected in creation myths, what, then, is the origin of such differences? Sanday argued that the explanation is to be found first and foremost in environmental circumstances (1981:especially chapter 3). Where basic societal dependency is upon animals, which males typically hunt or raise, women are rarely depicted as the ultimate creative power. Unpredictability and danger are inherent in such activities, with the result being an outer orientation, male-centered creation myths, and male dominance. Plant economies, on the other hand, especially the technologically simplest ones, reflect the typical femaleness of these activities through an inner orientation, with its ramifications for creation myths and sex-role plans. In short, "From their dependence people select their symbolism" (1981:72). In rooting the sex-role plan and cultural orientation of a society in the type of economy possible in a given environment, Sanday is not as removed from a general Marxist orientation as she may appear to be at first glance. Her emphasis is more cultural than that of the more explicitly Marxist approaches, but the logic of this theory is nonetheless materialistic in its basis. Indeed, in an earlier theory (1974), which she explicitly rejected in her 1981 book, Sanday argued for the primacy of economic and political variables in explaining gender inequality and viewed belief systems as functioning to legitimate the resulting gender stratification system. Her earlier, avowedly materialistic orientation has only been tempered, not abandoned in her later work.

In addition to considerations of food source, Sanday also argued that technological complexity, migration, and forces threatening to societal survival—be they other human collectivities or natural processes like food shortage—all enhance male dominance (1981:especially chapter 8). She summarized this by asserting that male dominance of women is a response to stress (1981:171–2). In such situations, societal survival rests more on male than on female actions, and for the sake of social and cultural survival, women accept male domination (1981:181–2).

This acceptance is not automatic: the extent to which the women of a society accept male dominance in response to stress is a function of their existing cultural metaphors.

> If a people's sex-role plan is part of a cultural configuration emphasizing cooperation, immersion of the group in nature, and the feminine principle, male dominance is unlikely to result unless the source of stress makes the fertility of women inimical to life itself. On the other hand, if a people's sex-role plan contains male and female principles, cooperation and competition, as is the case with the dual-sex cultural configuration, the stage is set for mythical male dominance. If both sexes have been traditionally associated with the sources of power, both will respond to stress by attempting to maintain their traditional power while striving to leave room for the other to maneuver. Finally, if the traditional sex-role plan is part of the "outer" configuration, women will become objects to be controlled in a game played by men for the purposes of men. (1981:186–7)

Women will struggle to protect their power base where preexisting cultural definitions support them, "unless men kill a few token women. . . . " Sanday concluded by asserting that

> if there is a basic difference between the sexes . . . it is that women as a group have not willingly faced death in violent conflict. That

fact, perhaps more than any other, explains why men have sometimes become the dominating sex. (1981:210–11)

Sanday also included in her theory a complicating dimension often ignored. She argued (1981:especially chapter 6) that in many societies apparent male dominance is balanced by female authority. Females may have economic or political authority based on either ascription or achievement. Where it is ascribed, it is a natural right rooted in "a long-standing magico-religious association between maternity and fertility of the soil [which] associates women with social continuity and the social good" (1981:114). In such societies, males will share authority based on their roles as hunters and defenders of the territory. In such cases, said Sanday, the likelihood that women's authority will diminish, due to socioeconomic stress or technological change, is low. Where women's authority is achieved, it is based on their role in the economy, where they are able to attain self-sufficiency and establish an independent sphere of control. Their authority is not, in this case, legitimated by a system of magicoreligious beliefs or legal titles and is therefore very vulnerable to reduction in the face of stress (1981:128).

To summarize briefly, Sanday argued that the proximate cause of gender inequality or male dominance is a sex-role plan, rooted in an outer orientation, as manifested by a creation myth in which males are dominant. The possible sources of this cultural configuration are several, especially an animal-based economy, societal stress, and a more highly developed technology. Where the cultural configuration places more emphasis on the feminine and inner orientation, women are better able to resist male dominance, even in the face of societal stress or social changes normally conducive to male dominance.

ROSALDO

Another central concern of traditional anthropology has been the family structure and kinship systems. Several feminist theories reflect this emphasis. In a paper that incorporated the ideas of major sociological theorists such as Durkheim, Parsons, and Simmel, Michelle Rosaldo (1974) developed a theory of gender inequality rooted in a conceptual distinction, which subsequently became widely used and debated by both sociologists and anthropologists. She grounded her theory in a distinction between the **domestic** and **public spheres** of social life, defining them as follows:

> "Domestic" . . . refers to those minimal institutions and modes of activity that are organized immediately around one or more mothers and their children; "public" refers to activities, institutions, and forms of association that link, organize, or subsume particular mother-child groups. (1974:23)

Rosaldo began by noting that, while there is certainly wide variation in the degree of gender stratification, "male, as opposed to female, activities are always recognized as predominantly important, and cultural systems give authority and value to the roles and activities of men" (1974:19). Moreover, while women often possess power, everywhere males surpass females in culturally legitimated authority (1974:21). She sought to understand both this constant phenomenon and also the obvious variation in the degree to which females are subordinated.

Rejecting biological determinism, Rosaldo located the source of the constant feature of gender stratification in the ways by which human cultures have responded to the biological facts of women's childbearing and lactating functions. These biological facts underlie an identification of women with domestic life and of men with public life.

> Although the fact that women give birth to and nurse children would seem to have no necessary entailments, it appears to provide a focus for the simplest distinction in the adult division of labor in any human group. Women become absorbed primarily in domestic activities because of their role as mothers. (1974:24)

Since men have no apparent commitment that is "as enduring, time-consuming, and emotionally compelling" as women's maternal commitment, they "are free to form those broader associations that we call 'society'" (1974:24).

Rosaldo then outlined a series of consequences of this gender-based division of labor (1974:24–35). Citing Chodorow's theory (1974), she delineated the personality differences that result in males and females (see the discussion of Chodorow later in this and the next chapters). She argued that men's distance from women and children allows them to develop an image of authority, integrity, and worth. Further, she posited that women's status is basically ascribed on the basis of their maternal function, where males must achieve a status in order to become men. Women's roles are thus relatively undifferentiated, while men's are differentiated and ranked in hierarchies. Yet another consequence is the association of which Ortner (1974; see later in this section) spoke, between maleness and culture, on the one hand, and femaleness and nature, on the other. Also, this gender-based division of labor results in a social perception of "women as anomalies" who do not fit in properly with the male-defined social order. Finally, female production, both process and product, is less public, less communally shared, than that of men. For all of these reasons, claimed Rosaldo, the division of labor that locates women in the domestic sphere and men in the public, produces gender inequality.

There are, however, differences in the degree of inequality. Rosaldo argued that the more firmly differentiated the two spheres, and the more women are isolated from one another and placed under a single man's authority in the home, the lower their status. Women are relatively more equal, then, where these spheres are only weakly differentiated (1974:36). Where they are highly differentiated, gender inequality is less under conditions where women enter the public world or men enter the home. In the first instance, there are also two possibilities. Women can enter the men's public world or they can create their own public world. She noted that the former strategy is usually effective for only a few, elite women. More commonly, where the domestic and public spheres are firmly differentiated, women win power and value by stressing their differences from men. Such differences can serve as the basis for female solidarity and the creation of extradomestic ties among women (1974:37, 39).

ORTNER

Another anthropologist, Sherry Ortner, concentrated exclusively on explaining the constant feature of female subordination described by Rosaldo. She looked to cultural definitions emanating from women's familial roles for an explanation (Ortner, 1974:69–71). Although related to Rosaldo's domestic-public distinction, Ortner concentrated on the dichotomy between **nature** and **culture**. She argued that women are everywhere identified more heavily with the former, men the latter. To varying degrees, all societies value culture more highly than nature, which is defined as a lower order of existence (1974:72). By culture Ortner meant:

> the process of generating and sustaining systems of meaningful forms (symbols, artifacts, etc.) by means of which humanity transcends the givens of natural existence, bends them to its purposes, controls them in its interest. (1974:74)

It is not that women are seen as natural, men as the opposite. Rather, women are viewed as having a more direct affinity with nature—a middle status between the two realms (1974:73, 84).

Ortner discussed three reasons for this gender-linked association. First, women's bodies seem closer to nature because of their reproductive and lactating functions. Women create "naturally"; men must express their creativity "artificially." In so doing, her creations are perishable, while his are relatively lasting, eternal, transcendent objects (1974:75). Citing Rosaldo, Ortner then claimed that women's physiological functions lead to their confinement to the domestic context. Infants and young children, as less-than-fully socialized members of the community, are perceived as closer to nature. Women's close association with children thus further links them to the realm of nature. Finally, Ortner cited Chodorow's discussion (1974; see sections later in this and the next chapter) of the psychic consequences of women's mothering to argue that women's psyche is perceived as closer to nature. Women's personality "tends to be involved with concrete feelings, things, people rather than with abstract entities" (1974:81). Moreover, women tend to be relatively more subjective than men. In turn, Ortner claimed that these traits are associated with the immanence and embeddedness of nature rather than the transcendence and transformation of culture.

All societies realize that women, as humans, also partake of the cultural. They are thus seen as standing midway between the two realms. Since all societies must socialize the young to become fully human, women as the socializers are seen as mediators between the realms of nature and culture. But the task of properly socializing the young is so important that the domestic unit must be closely controlled in order to ensure a proper outcome. Therefore, women come under the heavier restrictions and circumscriptions which surround that unit (1974:84–5).

> The result is a (sadly) efficient feedback system: various aspects of women's situation . . . contribute to her being seen as closer to nature, while the view of her as closer to nature is in turn embodied in institutional forms that reproduce her situation. (1974:87)

ORTNER AND WHITEHEAD

In a more recent paper, Ortner, along with Harriet Whitehead, suggested an idea that represents a relatively unique approach among feminist social scientific theories: that the gender system of a society is basically a prestige structure (1981:16). Working from Max Weber's discussion of status differentiation, they argued that prestige structures serve "as a screen between the various material, familial, and political structures that have been considered to impinge . . . upon cultural conceptions of manhood, womanhood, sex, and reproduction" (1981:13). In Weberian style, they carefully distinguished prestige—social honor, social value—from other dimensions (especially class) of social inequality. They recognized the empirical relatedness of the various dimensions and the vast differences among societies in the nature of such relationships. Prestige systems are expressed in various institutions, of which kinship affiliations are a very widespread type. A prestige structure is supported by symbols and beliefs that serve as a legitimating ideology (1981:15).

Ortner and Whitehead began their application of the prestige structures concept to gender with the assertion that "in every known society, men and women compose two differentially valued terms of a value set, men being as *men*, higher" (1981:16). In most societies, prestige hierarchies that pertain to dimensions other than the gender hierarchy, are, by and large, male games. The female's social position is, overwhelmingly, that of dependent or ward of her menfolk (1981:19). They argued that "gender concepts are functions of the ways in which male prestige oriented action articulates with structures of cross-sex relations." In other words, social definitions of gender flow from the extent to which and manner in which male prestige is related, *from the male point of view*, to the sexual division of labor, marriage, and consanguinity (1981:18). One looks to the consequences of these cross-sex structures for male prestige in order to understand their implications for women's relative status (1981:18, 20).

The authors applied their approach to a discussion of marriage and kinship. They argued that cultural definitions of femininity typically stress one kind of cross-sex relationship: either sister, mother, or wife. Which one is stressed is a function of the extent to which and ways in which male prestige hinges on marriage, or on sibling relations, or on filiation (1981:22). The specific type of cross-sex bond that becomes central to the definition of women (mother, wife, sister) is a function of its importance in generating or maintaining male status. Most frequently, this is marriage (wife). In turn, which type of cross-sex bond is made central to the definition of femininity shapes not only that relationship, but many other aspects of male-female relations (1981:23). For instance, where affinal relations (daughter-in-law, mother-in-law) are central, women are generally treated with less respect than in those cultures in which women are construed largely as kin (sisters, mothers). Conversely, where sibling definitions of womanhood are central, cross-sex relationships tend to be more equalitarian and less antagonistic (1981:23).

In summary, Ortner and Whitehead argued that in order to understand the gender system and women's place within it, one must first understand the basis for prestige among men in that society. What is not explained by this approach is why, in the first place, men's prestige needs take precedence in defining the gender system for both sexes. In effect, preexisting inequality is assumed and this becomes a theory of the reproduction of gender systems.

For technologically simple societies, environmental conditions are clearly important determinants of sociocultural phenomena. A concern with physical environment, and especially the kinds of subsistence economies possible in given environments, represent yet another set of issues traditionally considered by anthropologists. Such concerns have also been incorporated by feminist anthropologists, as we have already seen in Sanday's theory.

FRIEDL

Ernestine Friedl (1975) developed an account of the ways in which, and reasons for which, the status of women and men varies among hunting and gathering and horticultural societies, and an explanation of why men's status is always at least somewhat higher. She argued that the division of labor by sex varies depending on the natural ecology and subsistence base of the society. In turn, this has ramifications for how goods are distributed by their producers. Friedl asserted that when distribution and exchange occur outside the domestic unit, the reciprocal relations and obligations established serve as the basis of power. Distribution within the family unit does not result in the gain of such power resources.

In hunting and gathering societies (the subsistence bases that characterized all human societies until 10,000 years ago), men typically hunt large game and women gather plant food. Women are plant gatherers primarily because they spend most of their mature life pregnant or caring for (including carrying) young children, which prevents them from traveling the distances and at the speed required by large-game hunting. Meat gained from the hunt is both scarce and highly valued compared to foods that are gathered; therefore higher prestige accrues to hunters. Meat is also shared with the entire collectivity, while vegetable products are shared only within the domestic unit (1975:21–3). Thus, men, but not women, bind nonfamily members to themselves through the exchange of meat, in the process creating a superior power base. Because there is variation among societies in the extent to which men, relative to women, exchange sustenance extradomestically, there is variation in the extent of gender inequality. Such variation is primarily a function of the local natural habitat.

Among horticulturalists societal variability is even greater, but men tend to monopolize at least two interrelated things that involve them, more than women, in extrafamilial alliances: the clearing and allocation of land and warfare. They control land because of the potential threat of warfare from neighboring groups whose land theirs borders. Men constitute the warriors because they are biologically more expendable; the population can adequately reproduce itself with fewer males, but not if there are too few females. In turn, control of land and warfare make men more involved in extradomestic economic and political alliances than women, thereby creating gender inequality (1975:135).

HARRIS

In a similar vein, Marvin Harris developed a theory that links population pressure and resource shortage to the origins of warfare, female infanticide, and gender inequality (1978). He began by rejecting the view that humans or human males are innately aggressive. Yet, he also noted that, with very few exceptions, all known human societies have engaged in warfare. For simple tribal societies, warfare functions to disperse populations over a wider territory, thereby preserving natural resources necessary for group survival. Harris argued that pressure from growing population and inadequate resources eventually leads almost all societies into warfare (1978:38–9). Despite the fact that war produces casualties, not enough people die to have any serious impact on population pressure. Since the birthrate is always a function of the number of women in a society, population control is instituted through female infanticide. In turn, this practice is made possible, according to Harris, because the only way to rear men to be warriors is to devalue nonwarriors — women. Such devaluation results in neglect and abuse, as well as outright infanticide. To Harris, success at warfare in a technologically simple society is a function of the "relative number of brawny combatants" (1978:41). This would lead to a preference for males, but not an entirely male warrior band. Yet warfare almost everywhere is entirely masculine. Harris claimed that to entice males to be warriors, they must be rewarded with several wives and sexual privileges and taught to be fierce and aggressive. In turn, women have to be reared to define themselves as less worthy and powerful than men. It is the resulting gender hierarchy and self-definitions that keep women out of war (1978:42–3).

Let us look in more detail at Harris's analysis of gender inequality. He asserted that in all human societies, males have been at least somewhat superior to females in status and power, although the degree of inequality has been variable (1978:58–60). Warfare requires that communities be organized around a resident core of fathers, brothers, and their sons, which, in turn, results in the exchange of sisters and daughters between such groups. In this way, patrilineality, patrilocality, and bride price emerge. Harris also recognized, however, that some societies have been intensely militaristic, yet matrilineal, matrilocal, and relatively sexually equalitarian. He argued that such societies conduct **external warfare** in very large raiding parties against others far removed from the home territory. The men are thus absent for extended periods of time, and neighboring villages are allies. In their absence, women bear extensive responsibility.

> Shifts . . . to matrilineal organizations originate as an attempt on the part of absentee males to turn over the care of jointly owned . . . property to their sisters. Absentee males rely on their sisters rather than their wives because wives are drawn from someone else's . . . interest group and have divided loyalties. Absentee brothers . . . discourage marriages which would remove their sisters from the household . . . Sisters are only too happy to comply since patrilocal marriage exposes them to abuses at the hands of . . . husbands and unsympathetic [inlaws] . . . . (1978:61)

Yet even in such societies, "this modification of sexist hierarchy should not be confused with the nullification of that hierarchy" (1978:63).

Societies that follow the patrilineal, patrilocal, sexually more unequal pattern, which are the vast majority according to Harris, engage in **internal warfare**, fought by small bands against neighboring villages that probably share a fairly recent common ancestry. Nomadic and pastoral societies are almost always of this type also, because the entire community migrates with the men when they fight to expand their grazing territory (1978:60–62).

In summary, Harris was arguing that almost inevitably, population growth has produced resource shortages, which have produced warfare. Biology "destines males for training to be fierce and aggressive" because of their greater average size and strength. The payoff to men for risking their lives is female subordination, which renders even strong women unable to participate in warfare. But the extent to which females are subordinated is modified by the nature of the warfare itself.

SCHLEGEL

The final theory in this section is an eclectic one that reflects several of the traditional anthropological concerns we have seen in the theories already discussed. Alice Schlegel began by recognizing the wide diversity among societies in both the degree and types of gender stratification, which she defined as systematic (categorical) inequality on one or more of three dimensions: relations of material rewards, prestige, and power (1977:3). She argued that the degree of sexual inequality is a function of the importance of the roles played by each sex in their society's **central institutions**, but the specific institution(s) defined as central vary among societies. In turn, Schlegel defined a central institution "as one that establishes priorities in the allocation of time, goods, and personnel, and legitimizes motivation and justification for action" (1977:19).

Turning first to her discussion of the three dimensions of stratification, Schlegel noted that in simple societies that produce minimal surplus, prestige rather than material objects is the primary reward for the performance of highly valued social roles. Family members tend to share collective material assets relatively equally. Differential material rewards by sex tend only to occur when individuals, rather than families, control marketable skills or property, that is, in complex societies. In this case, if males possess greater access to skill development or property, there is extensive material sexual inequality (1977:6).

Playing highly valued roles, such as motherhood in many societies, does not automatically confer prestige. Schlegel pointed out that even when an object is valued, prestige goes only to those who own or control the valued object. Thus, if women are valued as objects in the social, political, or economic affairs of men, they will not have prestige (1977:7–8).

Her third dimension, power, entails two facets: the ability to control one's own person and activities (autonomy) and the ability to control others. They do not necessarily occur together (1977:8–9). A key aspect of power for determining gender stratification systems is the ability to control central institutions. Schlegel viewed power as the most important of the three dimensions, but argued that the other two cannot be ignored. In most instances, the three will be highly correlated.

Schlegel claimed that **sexual status**, presumably the combination of the three types of rewards, is a function of three broad institutional systems within society: the economic, social, and ideological (in some parts of her discussion she included power as a fourth; in other parts she subsumed it under the social). She began this part of her analysis by noting that men and women fill somewhat different roles in all societies, based on differences, and the social consequences of such differences, in reproduction (1977:23). In simple societies, the procreative system is of overriding importance in determining which tasks are best suited to men and women (1977:24). Those tasks that most efficiently articulate with motherhood are assigned to women, those that do so least to men. The household also functions as a productive unit in such societies, but economic relations do not usually dominate domestic ones. Both must be as fully accommodated as possible, so both function as central institutions. In advanced modes of production, specifically with industrialization, reproductive and productive tasks become isolated from one another. Economic units need not concern themselves with procreation. When this happens, the domestic sphere is demoted, leaving the economy as the central institution.

Schlegel argued that the division of labor by sex is the fundamental basis for gender stratification. But, she noted, while the sexual division of labor is necessary to produce sex inequality, it is not sufficient. Only when it becomes conjoined with central institutions controlled by men, as it typically does when the economy becomes the central institution, does gender stratification result from the sexual division of labor. However, this also happens in some simple societies.

In her discussion of the impact of the economic system on gender inequality, Schlegel emphasized the importance not of the division of labor per se, but of differential control over the means of production (1977:27–8). The social system, which includes power and authority relations, often affects control over the means of production. In simple societies, kinship usually constitutes the basic type of social bond. The sexual structure of the kinship unit (lineage, locality) in such societies often forms an important basis for determining power relations between the sexes:

> The kin group provides the major channels beyond the household through which loyalty is activated and social action is mobilized. Control over corporately held property, principles of inheritance of goods and positions, rights to form alliances through marriage – all of these are kinship features that can support or modify the power and authority of men and women gained through other means. (1977:29)

Other kinds of associations, that cut across family lines, can also serve as central social institutions. Such associations may deal with relations within society or external relations, and include military (almost always male), trading, and political groups. Where they serve as central institutions and are male dominated, gender stratification is more extensive (1977:29–30).

Schlegel argued against a Marxist position that defines ideological systems as simple reflections of economic or social relations. She recognized that there is indeed usually correspondence between an ideological system and social practice: between beliefs, symbols, and rituals concerning the sexes and their actual roles, behaviors, and relationships. She viewed this relationship as reciprocal, and thus argued that ideological systems must be treated as an independent variable in understanding specific systems of gender stratification (1977:31–4). She did not, however, explain the mechanisms by which ideology creates gender inequality.

In conclusion, Schlegel posited that variation in gender stratification systems is a consequence of the ways productive relations, social relations, and ideology are related to each other. The precise way these forces interact to produce specific systems of sexual status will differ according to both the internal dynamics of societies and their relationships to other societies (1977:353). But in all cases, the first place to look is to the central institutions of a society, to see whether and to what extent they are male dominated. In short, Schlegel rejected the possibility of a generally applicable theory that designates some variables as always having a given effect. Rather, she suggested that several broad categories of variables affect systems of gender stratification, and in each case one must examine empirically which type(s) is most important.

SUMMARY

Several common concerns and themes recur in the feminist anthropological theories reviewed, although no one specific perspective unites them in a coherent framework. First, all of these theories are overwhelmingly concerned with technologically simple, preclass societies, whose economies are primarily subsistence level. All claim that at least some minimal level of gender inequality exists in such societies. Because of the societies' technological simplicity, the environment plays a relatively important role in shaping social structure, especially through its impact on the division of labor by sex. In turn, most of the theories reviewed in this section stress the importance of that division of labor on the relative status of the sexes. A recurrent, but not uniform theme traces gender inequality to women's domestic and familial work, a theme encountered in the Marxist-feminist approach as well. Conversely, superior male status is viewed by most as rooted in their extrafamilial activities and group involvements. Another recurrent theme emphasizes the impact of environmental and social (e.g., warfare) stress on creating or exacerbating gender inequality. Finally, most of these theories consider cultural ideologies, and definitions of the valuable and important, as central variables in understanding the secondary status of women. The theories differ widely, however, in the importance granted to these various factors in producing systems of gender stratification and in the causal ordering of several of them.

ECLECTIC STRUCTURAL THEORIES

In this section, three macrotheories developed by sociologists will be reviewed. Each purports to explain gender stratification across societal types. That is, they claim that their theories embrace technologically and socially simple, as well as complex, societies. Each, therefore, was built upon anthropological, as well as sociological, data and theory. Although none represents one specific theoretical tradition, all three theories were substantially influenced by a general Marxist approach.

CHAFETZ

My own theory of gender stratification, *Sex and Advantage* (Chafetz, 1984; see also Chafetz, 1980a) was, in a very general sense, inspired by Marxist theory inasmuch as the primary explanatory variables concern the structure of economic activity. Several other types of variables also were used to explain the variation in the degree to which males and females are cross-culturally and historically unequal in their access to scarce and valued societal resources.

I began by noting two empirical facts: (1) that among known societies, the degree of gender stratification has varied from near equality to radical inequality favoring males; (2) that nowhere have females been systematically more advantaged than males. The explanation for the second fact can be deduced once the variation noted in the first is explained. In explaining the degree of gender stratification, I employed three sets of variables that are postulated as having direct effects (called intervening variables) and eight more (called independent variables) whose effects are indirect and mediated by those first three (see 1984:11 for a summary chart). The variables are related to each other systemically, meaning that they are all at least indirectly related to one another and that there are numerous feedback mechanisms. Thus, the theory simultaneously delineates the causes of variation in the degree of gender inequality and the mechanisms that tend to maintain such a system once in existence. In this chapter I will stress the causal mechanisms, reserving for the next chapter a discussion of those that function primarily to reinforce an existing status quo.

The most important variables are six which are clustered together under the rubric **Nature of Work Organization** (1984:especially chapter 3). The first of these refers to the extent to which women in a given society participate in work activities that are highly valued by their society. In nonsurplus-producing societies, such as hunting and gathering or simple horticultural ones, this variable refers to women's participation in the acquisition or production of food; in surplus-producing societies, to their contribution to surplus production of any commodity or service that can be exchanged with, or sold to, others. The second variable refers to the extent to which women workers can be easily replaced in their work, either by men or by a surplus pool of other women. A third dimension of work organization, and one closely related to the previous two, is the extent to which the two sexes engage in sharply sex-segregated work activities, that is, specialize in very different types of work. Fourth and fifth are the extent to which women control the means and products of their production. Such control is the single most important factor in the cluster of work variables (as it was for Marx). Finally, the attention span required of work activities will affect the extent to which women are involved in them, especially in preindustrial societies. In such societies, given that women are usually chiefly responsible for childcare, they often specialize in tasks that do not require lengthy attention spans and can be easily interrupted. Sex inequality is minimized where women produce those things highly valued in their society, are not easily replaced, often, ironically, because they work in highly sex-segregated occupations, and especially where they control the means and products of production.

The second most important cluster of variables refers to three components of family structure: lineage, locality, and the division of domestic labor (1984:especially chapter 4). My theory asserts that the way in which a society organizes its work activities profoundly influences family structure (a basic Marxist tenet), but a number of other variables also do this, including the system of gender stratification itself, social and religious definitions and stereotypes concerning gender, and the degree of environmental harshness or social threat experienced by a society. In turn, family structure exerts a strong effect on the manner in which the society organizes its work activities, thus indirectly affecting the degree of gender inequality. I postulate, in addition, a direct effect of family structure on gender stratification. In general, patrilineage, patrilocality, and a division of domestic labor that places maximal responsibility on women tend to arise from and reinforce a disadvantageous position for women in the nondomestic productive sphere. This produces extensive gender inequality, which in turn reinforces such a family structure. At the other extreme, matrilineality, matrilocality, and more extensive male involvement in domestic labor are related both to greater equality in the sphere of productive labor and to substantial social equality between the sexes.

The third set of variables that has a direct relationship to the degree of gender inequality is comprised of two social definitional variables: degree of ideological or religious support for gender inequality and degree of gender differentiation (stereotyping) (1984:especially chapter 2). The thrust of my argument, again reflecting a Marxian heritage, is that social definitions arise chiefly from the structures of work, family, and gender stratification, and in turn bolster such structures. Their primary importance is as mechanisms that legitimate hence help to maintain an existing system. Therefore, this part of the theory will be discussed further in the next chapter.

The eight independent variables in the theory directly affect one or more of the three clusters of intervening variables just described, thus indirectly affecting the degree of gender stratification (1984:especially chapter 5). Some are important chiefly in simple societies, others in all types. The extent of their impact is also variable.

Two important variables that have a strong impact on work organization refer to the average proportion of the female life cycle devoted to childrearing and the degree to which home and work sites are spatially separated. When women devote a large proportion of their lives to childrearing, either because of large families or because of very high per child investment, they are likely to be disadvantaged in the economy. But gender inequality in the economy is a major contributor to such high maternal investment to begin with. Where women perform valued economic functions, they tend to average few children, even in technologically simple societies. Where heavy maternal involvement is combined with extensive separation of home and work sites, women are especially disadvantaged. Particularly in simple societies, both the division of productive labor by sex and the extent of female participation are also influenced strongly by the degree to which extensive physical strength or mobility is required by work activities. The third independent variable refers to the fact that where the environment is naturally harsh, men tend to be more central to economic labor. In discussing these variables, I argued that it is not because women *can't* do certain work tasks. Rather, given sufficient numbers of people in the society, it is usually more *efficient* that men specialize in such tasks that remove workers from proximity to young children or require substantial strength. There is another kind of efficiency that prompts societies involved in extensive warfare to place higher value on males and to create systems of extensive gender inequality. Being biologically more expendable for species reproduction (as discussed by Friedl and reviewed in the last section), males are almost everywhere the warriors. In return for risking their lives, and in gratitude for protecting the collectivity, warriors, and by extension all males, are typically given a variety of perquisites in such societies. Other independent variables that have some impact are the relative societal emphasis on sustenance versus surplus or exchange production (females tend to fare best in sustenance economies where they typically provide a substantial share of the food), population density, and sex ratio.

The last of the eight independent variables is level and type of technology. The technology available to a society affects several of the other independent variables, and thus has a profound, although indirect effect on the work organization variables. For instance, it can affect birthrates, hence maternal involvement; it can affect the relative location of work and home sites and the physical strength and mobility requirements of work activities. I concluded that technology constitutes the single most important independent variable, and therefore that the degree of gender stratification in a given society at a given time is, first and foremost, the result of technological level and type. Technology does not affect gender stratification in a linear fashion: one cannot simply assert that the more sophisticated the technology, the more the level of sex inequality goes directly up or down. The long-term impact of the agrarian revolution was to increase gender stratification, of the industrial revolution to decrease it.

The heart of this theory is that technological level and type is the single most important determinant of the ways societies structure their productive work activities — their economies. In turn, the nature of work organization is the single most important determinant of the degree of gender inequality, both directly and through its impact on family structure and social definitions. Women as a general category have nowhere been superior to men in overall status because women have always been at least partially involved in domestic responsibilities. Where men monopolize economic activities, and women are solely responsible for the domestic realm, the sexes are radically unequal. The converse has never been reported. Where the two sexes more equally share economic activities, men tend to be more involved in the domestic sphere, and the sexes approach social equality (1984:21–2, 117–18).

BLUMBERG

Rae Lesser Blumberg has, over the course of more than a decade, developed a macrostructural theory of gender stratification in a series of papers, chapters, and a book. Her recent, fully developed version (1984) constitutes the basis of the discussion of her theory in this book. While this theory is eclectic in terms of the types of explanatory variables included, it focuses on the primary importance of the distribution of economic power in producing systems of gender inequality. In so doing, it too reflects a Marxist heritage, although it is not a Marxist-feminist theory (1984:25).

Like the Marxists, Blumberg posited that the most important determinant of gender inequality, meaning inequality in privileges, prestige, and freedoms, is women's ability, relative to men, to control the means of production and allocate surplus production. Such control is what she called **economic**

power (1984:47). She then asserted that the relative economic power of women varies, and not always in the same direction, at different social levels, such as the household, community, social class, and state (total society) (1984:25). Moreover, other forms of power, for example, force, political, and ideological, were viewed by Blumberg as less accessible to women and therefore not a simple outgrowth of economic power (1984:42). In fact, superior male power of these other types may prevent women from realizing the full benefits of their economic power. Nonetheless, the main pattern is that force, politics, and ideology appear weaker than economic power. In the absence of economic power, women have no access to other forms of power, although extensive economic power for women typically co-exists with superior (but not total) male power on these other dimensions. She concluded: "For women . . . the river of power does not flow two ways: the current goes from economic power to some degree of influence over the other spheres, rarely vice versa" (1984:46–7). Moreover, where it exists, that influence is not usually effective for women in achieving their own agenda: rather, it is a mediating force that can be used to veto or block men's use of power.

Perhaps Blumberg's most unique and important contribution to understanding gender stratification is her discussion of the **nesting system**, by which different societal levels control those below them. The lowest level, the household, is controlled by the community. In complex societies, above the community stands the class, above that the larger society, and today, possibly, above that the world economy (1984:48). Change in women's status and power may be introduced at any level; indeed women's relative power may improve at certain levels while it deteriorates in others. In general, the higher the level, the more important the noneconomic sources of power become.

Typically, males have been more dominant at the higher, more macrolevels. This fact functions as a **discount rate**, affecting women's ability to exercise their economic power at the lower or microlevels. By this Blumberg meant that women will not receive the full value of their economic power in the household and community because of male dominance at the class and societal levels. In short, women's actual micropower will be less than their potential power (1984:49). Moreover, in times of social change, men are apt to use their noneconomic sources of power, especially physical, to repress women, if they perceive change as threatening to their own relative position. From this perspective, widespread wife abuse and rape reflect social changes that are undermining male superiority. However, during times of stability, where women possess substantial economic power, even though it is discounted, they are less likely to be the victims of male power in other realms (1984:50–51).

What, then, determines the extent of women's relative economic power?

A precondition, but not a sufficient cause of economic power, is their participation in productive work. But it is only where women's work is of high **strategic indispensability** that they come to possess substantial economic power (1984:52). For Blumberg, it is not women's ability to *supply* labor that determines their economic power — it is the *demand* for their labor that does so (1984:54). The extent to which women provide strategically indispensable work, and hence come to possess economic power, is a function of a variety of things, including: the relative size of their contribution to total output; the **short-run substitution costs at the margin** of their labor (i.e., how difficult or costly it is to replace individual women workers); the extent to which they control technical expertise; the extent to which they work free from close male supervision; the degree to which they are able to collectively organize themselves (1984:57).

In addition to considerations of women's work, Blumberg argued that two other sets of factors affect the degree of women's economic power: kinship systems and the general stratification system of the total society. In the kinship system, the single most important factor is the pattern of inheritance: the more property women come to control through inheritance, the greater their economic power. Second, women's power is expedited by a residence pattern where they continue to live with their female kin after marriage, while patrilocality constitutes the least favorable system. Finally, matrilineal descent systems are most favorable, patrilineal least so, for the development of female economic power (1984:63–5). Two features of the class stratification system affect women's relative economic power. First, the more unequal it is, the more obstacles there will be to female economic power at the macro-levels of the society. Second, Blumberg argued that in class-stratified societies, the poorer the social class, the more equal in power are the sexes within that class (1984:67). In this way, Blumberg recognized that the degree of gender inequality is not uniform across all segments of complex societies.

To summarize Blumberg's central theoretical argument, the extent to which women and men are equal in prestige, privileges, and freedoms is primarily a function of their relative economic power. For women, the extent of their strategic indispensability in productive work roles is the most important determinant of their economic power, supplemented by the effects of several kinship and social stratification variables. To the extent that males dominate in other forms of power and at the macrosocial levels, female economic power tends to be discounted in terms of women's ability to convert it into privileges, prestige, and freedoms, even at the microlevels.

The final theory in this section was developed by Randall Collins, as part of a more general theory of social conflict (1975:chapter 5). He began by positing three constants concerning human beings: (1) that they have strong drives for sexual gratification; (2) that they strongly resist being coerced; and (3) that males are usually larger and stronger than females (1975:281). The combined effect of these three attributes is "that, without considering other resources, men will generally be the sexual aggressors and women will be the sexual prizes for men" (1975:230). Stated otherwise, men would use their superior coercive ability to control women, being motivated to do so by their strong sexual urges. If Collins stopped here, I would not consider including his theory in a book on feminist theory, since female subordination would be seen as the universal result of an immutable biological imperative.

Collins recognized, however, that there is variation among systems of gender stratification: despite the fact that male sexual property in women is the underlying cause of gender stratification, women's relative status is not a constant (1975:237). Variations in two structural features produce differences in systems of gender inequality: forms of social organization that affect the use of coercion and those that affect the market positions of men and women. The second feature reflects the basic Marxist approach already encountered in the other theories reviewed in this section. The first is uniquely concerned with the extent to which the political organization of a society constrains individuals from using force against one another. Collins argued that the two factors operate independently, which is different from traditional Marxist theory. He also considered a number of family features, which he treated primarily as intervening variables. These variables change first with the economic role played by women and secondarily with the level of force at the household level. In turn, family organization affects the status of women.

Maximal gender inequality occurs where males control both the means of violence and material resources. Women's relative economic resources, and hence overall social status, are best in nonsurplus-producing societies, where their work is central to the economic system, and where lineage and locality systems follow their sex. Where the political system concentrates force at the household level, women's relative position is worst (1975:282-3). Therefore, the development of nation states, which monopolize the legitimate means of coercion, has tended to reduce gender inequalities somewhat (1975:242-9). Further reduction (although not gender equality) occurs with the development of affluent market economies and the rise of widespread employment opportunities for women (1975:249-54).

In summary, Collins posited that the root cause of systems of gender stratification is the superior strength of males which, given the intense sexual urge of the species (including both sexes), men are motivated to use to control sexual access to women (see Blumberg, 1984, for a critique of this view). In short, female subordination is rooted in the biology of the species. Economic and political structures are then viewed as mitigating—in some cases extensively—this basic push toward female subordination, in a variety of circumstances.

EXCHANGE THEORY: PARKER AND PARKER

Seymour and Hilda Parker (1979) developed an Exchange theory of the causes of gender inequality that is based on an amalgamation of insights from biology, anthropology, psychology, and sociology. They began by noting that both the uniformity of male superiority cross-culturally and the diversity in the extent of such superiority must be explained by a theory of gender stratification. They rejected, at the outset of their paper, the idea that gender inequality is a result of biology *or* culture, rather seeking to develop a theory that integrates both, thereby avoiding the nature/nurture controversy.

The bulk of their paper is a review of findings on gender differences and the sexual division of labor from anthropology, from the infant and child development literature, and from biopsychological and primate studies. They concluded that the findings from these diverse sources converge, leading to the conclusion that there are indeed innate differences in the predispositions of the two sexes. Such differences constitute factors that take on meaning in a given experiential context (1979:299). The division of labor in hunting and gathering societies, which are characterized by a very simple technology, is explained largely by those biological differences. However, both quantitatively and qualitatively, females and males contribute equally to the subsistence and societal functioning in such societies. In short, the biologically rooted sexual division of labor does not automatically entail gender inequality. They raised the question, then, of how such differences become translated into inequality.

Exchange theory posits that people enter into and remain in relationships with others in order to maximize their material and nonmaterial rewards. Long-term, stable relationships entail the exchange of approximately equal values between parties. If one party has something of greater social value to exchange than the other, balance is maintained by the latter according greater power or prestige to the former. If the sexes are unequal, then from this theoretical point of view, males must have something of greater value than females to exchange, for which females have to grant males power and prestige in return. Parker and Parker argued that the different biologically rooted propensities of the two sexes result in a division of labor in simple societies in which male tasks require "strength, danger, achievement motivation, risk of failure and, relatively high levels of . . . training and skill." Female tasks, by comparison, are more "routine, repetitive, and relatively low risk, and did not require as high a mastery of technological skills" (1979:302). As a result,

> the requirements for male-role activities are elicited with greater difficulty or cost both to the individual and, therefore, to society. . . . The requisite skills for female-task performance are distributed more widely and evenly within the female population than are the requisite skills for male-task performance within the male population. (1979:300)

In short, male-task performance skills are more scarce and less easily substitutable. Therefore, they are more socially valued. In order to elicit male effort to achieve their tasks, society had to offer compensation, and such compensation comes in terms of granting them superiority in power and prestige over women. In addition, "the myth of male superiority was an element . . . that functioned to 'psych up' males—sustaining motivation to achieve in the face of danger and difficulty" (1979:302).

A continuous rise in the technological complexity of societies increased the specialized training, skills, and risks needed in men's work. This accounts for the widely noted fact that women's relative status is lower in technologically more sophisticated societies than in hunting and gathering ones—male superiority is seen as a compensation mechanism which maintains exchange balance.

Parker and Parker have developed a theory that argues that biological differences, within the context of a simple technology, have shaped the division of labor by sex. That division of labor was, however, asymmetrical in terms of danger and difficulty. Females have had to grant males superior power and prestige to equalize exchange relations. In their conclusion, the authors reminded readers that "there is no inevitable or direct causal chain that links biology to sociocultural phenomena" (1979:303). The Parkers' brief discussion of the ramifications of a highly sophisticated, modern technology on the division of labor and women's status is reviewed in chapter 5 of this book.

FEMINIST NEO-FREUDIAN THEORIES

CHODOROW

The only microlevel theories that explicitly attempt to explain the causes of gender inequality emanate from the Freudian tradition. In her award-winning book *The Reproduction of Mothering* (1978, see also 1974), Nancy Chodorow substantially revised classical psychoanalytic thought to reflect sociological insights and especially a feminist perspective. Her main thesis may be summarized as follows: By being the primary, indeed almost exclusive, caretakers of young children, women reproduce females who psychologically want to mother, men who are misogynistic and disinterested in nurturing children, and a system of gender inequality. This is primarily an issue of the maintenance of systems of gender inequality, which will be explored in more detail in the next chapter. Chodorow also recognized that the degree to which females have functioned as primary, not to mention exclusive, childrearers has been variable historically. While women always mother, the extent to which men participate in the nurturance of young children has differed. Therefore, the extent of gender inequality, which is rooted in the phenomenon of women's mothering, has been variable as well.

Chodorow claimed that while sex equality could exist, all previous and contemporary societies have in fact been male-dominated to a greater or lesser extent (1978:9–10). Her own theory did not actually specify the original or basic causes of such ubiquitous systems of inequality, beyond specifying that women always mother. She was careful to stipulate, however, that women's parental role reflects neither their biology nor intentional role training. She called upon several anthropological accounts (e.g., Rubin, 1975; Rosaldo, 1974; Ortner, 1974) to conclude:

> Women's mothering determines women's primary location in the domestic sphere and creates a basis for the structural differentiation of domestic and public spheres. But these spheres operate hierarchically. Kinship rules organize claims of men on domestic units, and men dominate kinship. Culturally and politically, the public sphere dominates the domestic, and hence men dominate women. (1978:10)

What we have here is circular reasoning concerning the basic causes of gender inequality. Women mother because they have been nurtured primarily by women. For the same reason, men are not nurturant. Women's mothering produces the very system of inequality that maintains the primacy of the mothering role for women. Having ruled out biology as the basis of women's mothering, how, then, did the system get its start? Why did not both parents equally nurture their children in simple societies? This problem of circularity underlies my earlier assertion that the primary utility of Chodorow's theory lies in its ability to explain the maintenance of a system of gender inequality, once such a system comes into being, not in its ability to explain the underlying causes of such a system.

KITTAY

Eva Kittay's theory introduced the concept of male **womb envy** as the counterpart of the Freudian concept of female penis envy. She defined womb envy broadly as male envy of "the complex of a woman's organs and capacities, particularly as it relates to her distinctive childbearing functions" (1983:95). Kittay appeared to claim that this phenomenon is universal. She also argued that it stands at the root of systems of gender inequality, which she likewise saw as universal. Nonetheless, as I shall discuss in chapter 5, Kittay believed that it is possible to produce males without womb envy and thereby to create a system of gender equality.

Womb envy, while rooted in the inability of males to have babies, is nonetheless culturally, not biologically, produced according to Kittay. Like Chodorow, she began by pointing to the intense identification and close affectual ties of children of both sexes with their mothers as primary caretakers. This, in turn, creates in children a desire to mother — to bear and nurture their own children. Some time between ages five and seven, boys come to understand that they can never become mothers. Simultaneously, they discover that males have superior social status and power. At that point, a boy comes to a realization

> that he would possess mother's birth-giving powers only at the expense of his superior position which is equivalent to his masculinity, and which, in turn, stands in direct opposition to the femininity of his mother, which makes her at once capable of giving birth and a devalued person. (1983:104)

She suggested that his response is to revalue and devalue birthgiving. This is a defense mechanism for dealing with the envy, but it ultimately fails to compensate for the loss (1983:105).

The specific defenses by which womb envy is handled vary according to the cultural and the material life of the society. But regardless of their form, "envy is a destructive emotion that tends to spoil the very thing it covets" (1983:105). Envy results in angry and destructive feelings and actions directed against women, the possessors of the desired object.

Kittay then discussed six specific types of defenses against envy: (1) idealization (as in sentimentalizing motherhood while reducing all women to that role); (2) devaluation of the object (such as defining women's bodies, their sex organs, or the process of birth as repulsive); (3) devaluation of the self; (4) appropriation (as when men "give birth" to ideas, art, etc.; male initiation ceremonies, couvade rituals where males symbolically give birth along with their wives; male appropriation of the birthing process in modern medicine); (5) stirring up envy in others; and (6) stifling feelings of love and intensifying those of hate (towards women and children, as reflected in violent pornography, for example) (1983:105–20). It would appear from her discussion that female subordination is probably most heavily the result of defenses two (devaluation), four (appropriation), and six (stifling love, intensifying hate). Two and six are obvious in their ramifications. When Kittay spoke of appropriation, she pointed out that the activities involved only serve . . . envious impulses when they exclude women or deny her agency, so that they can be thought of as exclusively or primarily male domains in which men outdo women with respect to that which they envy in women's power. (1983:115)

In her conclusion, she argued that for most boys, the likely outcome of womb envy is

forming ambitions in which he can outdo women in their productivity, accepting ideologies in which men play the "really" important part in procreation and the family and, in general, fiercely adopting the stance of male superiority. (1983:121)

RUBIN

Yet a different kind of neo-Freudian approach is represented by anthropologist Gayle Rubin's (1975) essay, which attempted to integrate and reinterpret two theorists in a feminist light: Freud and French Structural anthropologist Claude Lévi-Strauss. Her rendition of Lévi-Strauss's ideas is central to explaining the root causes of systems of gender inequality. The Freudian ideas she employed are used primarily as mechanisms to explain the maintenance and perpetuation of such systems. Although she is included among the neo-Freudian feminist theorists, that aspect of her theory will be explicated in the next chapter.

To Rubin, as to Lévi-Strauss, society and culture are rooted in an exchange of women as marital partners. Such exchanges contributed to the very creation of society, because they bound together those who were not blood kin. In other words, women came to function as the cement linking families into kinship networks and social collectivities. But, Rubin noted, women cannot serve this function unless men already have the right to dispose of their female kin. The question of how men gained such power in the first place is not answered.

From Rubin's perspective, taboos against incest and on the division of labor by sex (that men not do whatever is defined as women's work, and vice versa) arise in order to ensure marital exogamy. Incest taboos serve to preserve females for exchange with other families. At least as fundamental are division of labor taboos, which divide the sexes into two mutually exclusive categories, thus radically extending very minimal biological differences and creating gender. Given a sexual division of labor, each sex is dependent upon the other and is incomplete without a partner. Rubin argued that "the division of labor can also be seen as a taboo against sexual arrangements other than those containing at least one man and one woman, thereby enjoining heterosexual marriage" (1975:178).

To the extent that the exchange of women is a fundamental feature of social life, the sexual division of labor is asymmetrical: the exchanger (males) and the exchanged (females) are not equal. Rubin argued that this asymmetry requires control over female sexuality specifically. Thus, some degree of gender inequality is deeply rooted in the fundamental nature of human society as a collectivity of kinship networks brought about by the exchange of women as mates. However, why women and not men were exchanged is not explained by this theory and hence inequality is more presupposed than explained.

SUMMARY AND CONCLUSIONS

In this chapter explanations have been reviewed that reflect widely diverse theoretical traditions. Yet basic similarities may be discerned among them in their attempts to explain why gender inequality arose or exists. Generally speaking, the various approaches begin by looking to the relationship between women's biological functions as childbearer and lactating feeder, on the one hand, and the subsistence or economic basis of the society, on the other, to understand how human communities structure the division of labor by sex. Given a particular type of economy and women's biological functions, a specific, gender-based division of labor arises that is *apparently efficient* for the collectivity or for those who control the economy. The major location of this division of labor is the family, which thus assumes fundamental importance in virtually all theories of gender stratification. But as a few theorists have explicitly recognized, the fact that males and females do *different* work is not automatically the same as positing *inequality*. Indeed, some theorists have noted that a gender-based division of labor makes the sexes mutually dependent upon one another and thereby undergirds heterosexual marriage. To move from the division of labor to gender stratification some mechanism(s) must be specified that translates differentiated work into a hierarchical arrangement. It is here that the theories diverge from one another.

The Marxist-feminists posit that a gender-based division of labor arises in class, and especially in capitalist societies, by which males provide subsistence for their wives and children, resulting in extensive economic dependency of women on men. It is unequal economic power, rooted primarily in the behavior of economic elites, that explains gender stratification from this perspective. The same general approach is shared by some anthropologists and the eclectic macrostructural theories, which likewise stress the centrality of economic power to an explanation of gender inequality (e.g., Blumberg, Chafetz).

Some of the theorists emphasize, or at least include, forms of power other than economic as important for transforming a division of labor into a system of inequality. The power of men to physically coerce women figures prominently in Collins's theory and in a secondary manner in Blumberg's. The male role in warfare also is posited by several as playing a significant role in creating or exacerbating sex inequality (e.g., Harris, Chafetz, Friedl, Sanday).

A somewhat different answer to the question of how "different" becomes "unequal" is offered by an Exchange perspective. One explicit example of this was given, yet some of the other theories (e.g., Harris) implicitly assume the same perspective. In an Exchange approach, something about the gender-related tasks (e.g., their danger, arduousness, or skill level) is said to differ, such that women must supplement their contribution of labor in order to make the exchange with men fair. They do this by deferring to males in terms of power or prestige. This differs from the Marxian-based explanations primarily in terms of what is unequally exchanged. At heart, the Marxian theories are also Exchange theories, arguing that men and women do not exchange equally in the economic realm and therefore men acquire power. The theories labeled here as Exchange focus on unequal exchange of noneconomic aspects of labor. Another variant of an Exchange approach is also represented in the theories reviewed. In this variant the argument is made that the activities specific to males involve them in exchanges with members of other kin groups, while women only exchange within their own families. In this fashion, men build reciprocal obligations, alliances, and a power base across families. This power base is unavailable to women except through their relationships to particular men (e.g., the theories of Friedl, Rubin, Rosaldo).

A very different kind of answer is offered by the neo-Freudian feminists. To them, the fact that the division of labor makes women the primary child-rearers of both boys and girls has long-term, largely unconscious, and very different effects on the basic personality structures of males and females. These differences then prompt males to devalue females.

Cultural values and ideologies (including religion and myth) play a role in most of the theories reviewed. Their relative power to cause gender inequality is certainly disputed. However, the assertion that systems of gender stratification are in some fashion intertwined with, undergirded by, or legitimated by cultural values and ideologies, is widely accepted. Several theories explicitly discuss these dimensions (e.g., Sanday, Sacks, Vogel, Ward, Chafetz). Explanations (such as Schlegel's and Ortner and Whitehead's) that use the prestige dimension of gender stratification are implicitly concerned with cultural values, since the very meaning of prestige concerns activities or statuses defined as valuable by the members of a collectivity.

The theories reviewed in this chapter suggest one inescapable conclusion: any given gender stratification system is deeply embedded in the entire complex of institutions, beliefs, and practices that characterize its society. In the next chapter the complex relationships between gender systems and other socioeconomic, cultural, and social psychological phenomena will be further underscored as we examine a number of explanations of how such systems are maintained and reproduced.

3 MAINTENANCE AND REPRODUCTION OF GENDER SYSTEMS

Undergirding any system of inequality, and especially one based on ascription, is the assumption by most societal members that unequally ranked categories are comprised of people who are fundamentally different from one another. In the last chapter we saw how differences in the gender division of labor have been used by a variety of theorists to account for inequality between the sexes. It has been postulated by social theorists that males and females differ in other ways as well. In this chapter, two separate but related issues are the central focus of several theories: How are gender differences created and intergenerationally transmitted? How do such differences, or the belief in differences, function to sustain and reproduce systems of gender stratification?

The concept of gender difference is comprised of two distinct aspects: real or measurable differences and the belief systems about differences. Real or observable differences between the men and women of a given society, on the average, occur in such things as personality attributes, intellectual functioning, values, and so on. By adulthood, people's personalities, intellects, values, and behaviors are thoroughly infused by gender—people are **gendered**. Some theories seek to explain the social and interpersonal processes that generate such differences in each generation. This is preeminently a microlevel issue. To the extent that such differences exist, another theoretical question entails explaining how they become relevant to sustaining a system of unequal access to power, wealth, and prestige. This is an issue that bridges the micro- and macrolevels. Cultural belief systems concerning gender differences may or may not be congruent with reality. Regardless, they affect the expectations and behaviors of societal members and therefore the opportunities available to males and females. This is a more specifically macrolevel issue.

Finally, there are social practices and structures—especially normative, ideological, and power structures—which are conceptually independent of (although related to) issues of gender differences, that function to bolster any system of inequality, including gender stratification. Such phenomena are manifested at the level of interpersonal relations between the sexes and thus constitute a concern of some microtheories. They are also fundamental features of social collectivities and thus constitute major focii of the macrotheories. chapter 3 will begin with the macrolevel and macrostructural theories and end with the microinteractional.

MARXIST-FEMINIST EXPLANATIONS

The Marxists-feminists discussed in the last chapter have stressed the interdependence and mutual supportiveness of capitalism and patriarchy, though they have not devoted specific attention to exploring the processes by which systems of gender inequality are maintained. (A clear distinction is not made in most of the Marxist-feminist theories between the issues of focus in chapters 2 and 3.) In stressing the mutual relatedness of capitalism and patriarchy, Marxist-feminists have argued that capitalists profit from women's oppression and are thus motivated to develop and support policies, practices, and ideologies which sustain patriarchy. The specific nature of such actions by capitalists vary over time and space, as the nature of capitalism itself varies. Because capitalists constitute the ruling class, which controls political and cultural as well as economic institutions, they presumably possess the power to realize their aims quite effectively. Moreover, they will generally be supported by working class men, who also profit from a system of gender inequality even while suffering exploitation under a capitalist system. For male workers, both the necessary labor that maintains the workers and is provided by women in their domestic roles and their competitive advantages over women in the wage labor market serve as powerful incentives to support sexism (see especially Hartmann, 1979).

HARTMANN

The theory propounded by economist Heidi Hartmann exemplifies both the issues discussed in the last chapter and, relative to other Marxist-feminists, a somewhat more explicit emphasis on the issues of concern in this chapter. Like the others, she argued that the sexually based division of labor, which has existed in almost all societies, constitutes the basis of patriarchy, which by logical deduction must also have existed in virtually all societies. Hartmann did not explore the origins of these phenomena, however, but focused on the dynamics of patriarchy and its relationship to capitalism.

Hartmann defined patriarchy

> as a set of social relations between men, which have a material base, and which, though hierarchical, establish or create interdependence and solidarity among men that enable them to dominate women. Though patriarchy is hierarchical . . . [men] are united in their shared relationship of dominance over women; they are dependent on each other to maintain that domination. . . . men . . . are bought off by being able to control at least some women. (1984:177)

She argued that the material base upon which patriarchy rests is, first and foremost, men's control over women's labor, which allows men to exclude women from access to some essential productive resources. Male control over female sexuality is a secondary base of patriarchy. By controlling women's access to resources and their sexuality, men control women's labor power for the purpose of serving men in many personal and sexual ways, as well as for the purpose of rearing children. In turn, as childrearers, women reproduce patriarchal social relations intergenerationally, supported in this by other social structures such as churches, schools, sports, clubs, unions, armies, factories, offices, health centers, and the media (1984:178).

The partnership of patriarchy and capitalism can be traced historically to the development of a **family wage** in the early twentieth century. The family wage refers to male wages sufficient to support a dependent wife and their offspring. The concept of a family wage has resulted in lower wages for others, such as young people and women, enforced by job segregation in the labor market, and supported by both unions and management. Low wages for women mean that they will be more inclined to choose careers as full-time housewives, thereby providing a variety of services to men. In turn, women's home responsibilities reinforce their inferior labor market position. As housewives, women also serve capitalism as consumers. The wage differential between the sexes reinforces the familial division of labor and women's economic dependency on men (1984:182–4). The family wage establishes a familial structure that allows men to control women's labor within the family and outside of it.

Hartmann then turned her attention to the ideological justification that simultaneously legitimates both capitalism and patriarchy. She argued that the major characteristics that define masculinity are the same as the dominant values of capitalism: competitiveness, rationality, domination. These traits function to glorify maleness and capitalism. Simultaneously, female charac-teristics and social need are denigrated (1984:186–7). Those jobs considered appropriate for women (e.g., teacher, welfare worker) often entail nurtur-ance and serve social needs, both devalued under patriarchal capitalism. Therefore, the jobs are devalued and poorly paid, and social needs are inade-quately met.

From Hartmann's perspective, gender inequality is maintained and trans-mitted through the generations because capitalism has joined forces with patriarchy to dominate women's labor and sexuality. Low wages tie women to marriage and the domination of men, who have higher wages. In turn, the obligations of the wife role reinforce low wages. An ideology justifying both patriarchy and capitalism legitimates and reinforces women's oppression.

DOMESTIC ISOLATION

From a Marxian perspective, the development of a revolutionary or change-oriented consciousness occurs when deprived people come into contact with one another, communicate, and thus come to discover and understand their collective deprivations and the social structural causes of them. The isolation of households in modern societies precludes the development of such con-sciousness among women, rendering those who are confined to the domestic sphere the unwitting supporters of the very institutions that suppress them. As Karen Sacks suggested:

> Because of their isolation and exclusion from the marketplace, women can be used as a conservative force, unconsciously uphold-ing the status quo in their commitment to the values represented by home, family, and children. (1974:221)

Women thus come unwittingly to serve as important agents of their own op-pression. Ending the domestic isolation of women constitutes a necessary first step in a more general process of change toward gender equality, a topic discussed in the final chapter on social change.

ECLECTIC STRUCTURAL THEORIES

Eclectic structural approaches vary in their level of analysis and in the aspect of structure upon which they concentrate. In this section I begin with several theories that concentrate on the highest macrolevel: the society. Subse-quently, theories that focus on the institutional level, specifically the family and the economy, are examined. I end with one theory that addresses the for-mal organization. The structural variables that recur most frequently in these theories include ideological and normative systems and authority and power relations.

When I reviewed my own theory of sex inequality (Chafetz, 1984) in the last chapter, I said that it was systemic and therefore involved many feedback relationships. From this theoretical perspective, a system of gender stratification emerges first and foremost from the way productive work is organized by sex, and secondarily from family structure. However, once in existence, such a stratification system functions to reinforce family and economic structures. For instance, when women are socially disadvantaged and devalued, people will want to define themselves through their more prestigious male ancestors and men will favor their sons in inheritance, thus reinforcing patrilineage. When men are socially advantaged, they will have the power to exclude women as competitors for jobs, thus reinforcing women's lack of participation in the economy or their confinement to less valued work.

Beyond such feedback, the theory specifically postulated two social definitional variables as functioning primarily to legitimate and reinforce an existing gender stratification system (1984:especially chapter 2). The first of these is the degree of gender differentiation by which is meant "the extent to which . . . societal members . . . expect males and females, on the basis of their categorical membership, to manifest different traits of behavior, personality, intellect, and interest" (1984:24), in other words, gender stereotyping. I argued that such stereotypes arise when males and females play very different social roles in the economy and family. In turn they reinforce that division of labor by specifying different competencies for each sex.

But since different is not the same as unequal, by themselves, gender stereotypes cannot legitimate a system of inequality. To do so a broad idea system is required, which helps its adherents to interpret and give meaning to their lives as individuals and as parts of a community. Such idea systems are called ideologies if they are secular and religions if they pertain to the sacred. In the Marxist tradition, I viewed them as arising out of and reinforcing a structural reality rooted chiefly in economic organization. Therefore, ideological and religious pronouncements relevant to gender — the roles, rights, obligations, statuses of women and men — will reflect the social structural status quo, including in addition to work organization, the sex ratio, the frequency of warfare, family structure, and the gender stratification system itself. If women are severely disadvantaged relative to men, the dominant religion or ideology of that society will tend to justify that disadvantage by defining it as right and proper in terms of a larger principle, such as God, the masses, or the nation-state.

To justify gender inequality, males and females must be perceived as both different and differentially meritorious. Those who profit from such a system of inequality (men) are highly motivated to justify and legitimate it. When inequality is legitimated, the disadvantaged become more willing to accept

Maintenance and Reproduction of Gender Systems   71

their subordination and therefore less likely to challenge the status quo. The social definitional system thus arises out of a given socioeconomic structure and strongly reinforces it by legitimating it, according to this theoretical approach. Once in existence, idea systems often become quite strong and resistant to change. In an era of social structural change, they therefore tend to work for the conservation of the old system and typically lag behind other societal changes.

GUTTENTAG AND SECORD

In their award-winning book *Too Many Women?*, Guttentag and Secord explored the effects of a mostly ignored macrostructural variable, **sex ratios**, on the relative status and treatment of women (1983:especially chapters 1 and 9). They explicitly presupposed a system of gender inequality (which they termed inequality of **structural power**), then asked what happens when the sex ratio departs substantially from 100 (i.e., when there is a surplus of one sex). Common sense might lead one to suppose that sex ratios are both something over which humans exercise little or no control, and that they usually hover around 100 for total communities or populations. However, Guttentag and Secord demonstrated marked skewness in sex ratios in many times and places, as well as explicating several sociocultural variables that tend to produce markedly high or low sex ratios. Implicit in their theory is the argument that skewed sex ratios reinforce female disadvantage. Their explicit focus, however, was on the very different effects of skewed sex ratios on male-female dyadic relationships, depending on whether the sex in surplus is male (a high sex ratio of over 100) or female (a low sex ratio of less than 100).

Guttentag and Secord argued that in high sex ratio societies, since women are scarce, they are highly valued. Young women are valued for their beauty and glamour, married women as wives and mothers. Because of their scarcity, men compete with each other to win and keep a woman. Chivalrous and protective codes of behavior are typical. In such situations, women achieve substantial dyadic power with their husbands. However, given that men have considerably more structural power than women, men are able to respond to a scarcity of women by institutionalized means of monopolizing one. The result is that in high sex ratio societies, there is a premium on female monogamy and a protective morality that limits women's interactions with men and shapes female roles in the domestic direction. In short, the very high value placed on women by men, because of their scarcity, results in a system of tight control over them, given a preexisting system of male power.

In the converse situation, where males are scarce yet command more structural power, they devalue women, express misogyny, fail to make permanent commitments to women, and exercise strong dyadic power in relationships with women. Women are treated as sex objects, and adultery and divorce are common. However, because they can't rely on a man, in such situations women are likely to become more economically and otherwise independent. Indeed, Guttentag and Secord saw low sex ratios as a major cause of feminist movements. While in general there is a decline in emphasis on female domesticity, nonetheless some women will go to extra effort to attract or keep a man, making sacrifices and going out of their way to please him (1983:21).

I interpret Guttentag and Secord's argument to mean that, given a system of gender stratification, women's disadvantages are exacerbated by skewed sex ratios, although in different ways, depending on the direction of skewness. When they are scarce, women are so highly valued that they become tightly controlled in fear of their loss. However, they are unlikely to perceive their gender-based disadvantages because of the apparent esteem in which they are held, their dyadic power, and their security within marriage. When they are in oversupply, women gain some measure of autonomy at the expense of being despised and mistreated. In this instance, women are prone to unhappiness, a perception of the fact of inequality, and collective action in opposition to it. Nonetheless, there is no indication that in either case is male superiority in structural power seriously threatened. It should be noted in conclusion that Guttentag and Secord presented an entirely different scenario of the effects of skewed sex ratios in a context of female superiority in structural power. But this scenario is presented as purely hypothetical, since they asserted the universality of gender inequality favoring males up to the present time.

HOLTER

Norwegian sociologist Harriet Holter published one of the earliest analysis of gender differentiation and stratification (1970) to appear after the reemergence of feminism as a social movement in the late 1960s. While not an integrated theory, *Sex Roles and Social Structure* contains a variety of theoretically insightful analyses that address the issues of concern in this and the next two chapters (1970:especially chapters 1 and 10).

Holter began by defining **sex differentiation** as "a set of norms requiring individuals with given attributes to perform certain tasks or conferring given privileges on them" (1970:18). Sex differentiation is one of several societal distributive systems, all of which

> depend for their maintenance on a complex interaction between ideologies and power relations—economic, social, and psychological—produced by the distribution. Any principle of distribution is justified by beliefs or ideologies, and beliefs serve partly as motivating forces for engaging in the required role behavior. (1970:19)

Maintenance and Reproduction of Gender Systems   73

Systems of task or role differentiation produce systems of stratification, or inequities in power, authority, or prestige, because some tasks typically give greater access to resources than do others. Such a process is in part hidden, in part counteracted in sex differentiation by the special emotional and psychological dependence of each gender on the other (1970:22).

Distributive systems may be achievement or ascription based—sex differentiation is the latter. Holter argued that more than achieved attributes, ascribed ones are a fixed part of the individual's identity and psychological functioning, because they are learned from the very outset of life. This makes differentiation rooted in ascription, such as gender, more resistant to change than achievement-based differentiation (1970:20). Indeed, Holter argued that early socialization to sex roles is a primary means of maintaining current standards of sex differentiation (1970:214).

In order for an ascription-based system of differentiation to survive, at least one of three conditions must be met, according to Holter:

(1) evidence or belief that there are in-born individual differences in capacities associated with the given ascriptive attribute;
(2) belief in differentiation as a natural or a sacred, God-given law;
(3) evidence or belief that the system . . . increases efficiency. (1970:21)

At least some minimal rewards must be offered for the fulfillment of ascriptive role obligations if people are to be motivated to conform. In their absence, however, ascriptive-based differentiation can be maintained and reinforced by coercion. Dissatisfaction resulting from sex or other ascriptive differentiation may become widespread. However, the system will be attacked only if the dissatisfied come to believe that the system of differentiation itself, and not some other circumstance, is the cause of their problems (1970:21). Such a belief necessitates that members of a dissatisfied sex consider it appropriate to compare themselves to members of the other sex. Logically, then, a major mechanism in support of gender systems is an ideology embracing one or more of the three elements listed above. Such an ideology would preclude the kind of comparisons necessary to even contemplate attacking the system.

Societies tend to define either ascription or achievement as the legitimate, just basis for differentiation and stratification. Where ascription is regarded in this fashion, the gender system is reinforced. However, societal values that stress achievement contradict gender systems. In such contradiction lies a potential seed of change (see chapter 5). In a later paper Holter (1972) developed this theme further. She argued that contemporary industrial societies are characterized by a general ideology of equalitarianism. Given such an ideology, it is no longer possible to have openly recognized and accepted differentiation that is expressed in laws or other codes. Social ideology and the reality of women's status become discrepant, unlike traditional societies in which ideology, the division of labor, and personality formation were substantially harmonized for each sex (1972:336–8).

How is gender inequality maintained in light of such discrepancy? Since legal sanctions cannot be used against deviants, informal mechanisms must be employed. Holter located as the most critical informal mechanism psychological sex differentiation. She argued that task differentiation between men and women, and the resulting system of gender inequality, now depend on the formation of different personalities in boys and girls, and on teaching members of both sexes the importance of conformity (1972:338). In turn, the emphasis on psychological differentiation is legitimated by reference to scientific research, which has replaced religion as the primary ideological justification of gender differences. In addition, the discrepancy between a general ideology of equality and the reality of gender inequality is covered up by a tendency to increase women's influence in institutions that are becoming obsolete (e.g., the family, certain types of jobs, and some political offices). Finally, Holter argued that covert discrimination against women results in their feeling defeated and inadequate, precisely because they are given the illusion that they are equal to men. Women thus come to devalue themselves.

Fox

Holter's emphasis on the importance of gender-based personality differentiation for maintaining contemporary systems of sex inequality has been further elaborated in the work of Greer Litton Fox (1977). She began by describing three types of systems different societies use to control the behavior of women. **Confinement** refers to the restriction of women to the boundaries of the home, as in systems of purdah. **Protection** is a system where women have access to the world beyond the home, but only when accompanied by a chaperone. Both obviously limit women's ability to engage in the same types of activities as men in the public world and thereby help to sustain a system of gender inequality. The focus of Fox's analysis, however, was on the third type, which has characterized much of the Western world including the United States. She called this type **normative restriction**. In this system, from the beginning of life females internalize self-regulatory values and norms concerning what "nice girls" or ladies do and do not do. In all contexts, with members of both sexes, throughout the entire life span, pressure exists to live up to such standards. Since the ideal of niceness is not class specific, every woman is expected to act like a lady. Moreover, niceness attaches to behavior, not to the individual. It is therefore continually in jeopardy; to be a lady is to constantly act nice (1977:809).

Fox then traced the implications of a normative system of control over women. She noted that restrictions on travel, modes of travel, times of travel (daylight only when unaccompanied), entrance into certain places (e.g., bars), sexuality, and types of jobs (e.g., dirty work or work in dirty places) result from it. Certain types of work (white collar), in certain types of settings (offices), with certain types of co-workers or clientele (white collar, college educated, polite) support an image of niceness; others do not. Moreover, this form of social control "has the virtue of subtlety: it gives the appearance of nonrestriction and noncontrol, thus reducing the potential for resistance" (1977:816). Failure to maintain the image of nice is the fault of the individual, who can presumably control her own behavior. Therefore, whatever negative sanctions she receives, she will have earned.

Women who comply with such normative controls are guaranteed "safe passage in the world." Fox described the costs of conforming, however: "Normative restriction limits a woman's personal freedom . . . with the attendant cost of information control, and lays the groundwork for a circumscription of women's . . . power and control in the world" (1977:816–7). Because of it, women are channeled into jobs that fail to use their full range of skills and capacities. More than this,

> the nice girl value construct also keeps women out of men's way. By limiting women's power and degree of participation in the public world, by channeling women into certain jobs, by limiting the expression of female sexuality, and by providing a ready justification for punishment, the nice girl construct can be seen to facilitate the hegemony of men in a sex-stratified world. (1977:817)

LIPMAN-BLUMEN

If one set of societal norms serve to instill in females motivations to behave in ways that maintain their disadvantage, are there analogous processes that aid males in maintaining their advantages? Jean Lipman-Blumen (1976) posited that gender inequality is maintained and reproduced through male **homosociality**. This term is defined as "the seeking, enjoyment, and/or preference for the company of the same sex" (1976:16). She applied this to males, arguing that from boyhood on, they are attracted to, stimulated by, and interested in other males. Women have not been homosocial, at least until the recent advent of feminism. In fact, they have been more oriented to males than to other females because they find other women less interesting and useful than men. This difference results from a psychological tendency for people to identify with others whom they perceive to be the controllers of resources. In a system of gender inequality, women must seek to have their needs met, to gain resources, through men. In turn, women "become resources which men can use to further their own eminence in the homosocial world of men" (1976:16). Lipman-Blumen argued that females fashion themselves as sex objects in order to attract male attention away from other men. Nonetheless, men remain attracted to the homosocial world long after they become engaged in heterosexual relationships.

Homosociality among men limits women's access to and reinforces men's control of all important social institutions, including law and law enforcement, politics, the military, and the economy. Women derive their status through men and unwittingly perpetuate the system by marrying men who have higher status than they do. Children become, for women, a means to bind men to them, yet children serve to further reduce women's access to other resources.

> Thus . . . the different institutions . . . all act in an integrated and reinforcing way to maintain a male homosocial world in which only men are included and allowed access to the various resources of a society. . . . Women, children, and men who cannot meet the strict criteria of the male homosocial world are excluded and [for them] . . . it is virtually impossible to accumulate resources that would set them free. (1976:24)

Lipman-Blumen argued that this system is powerfully reinforced by traditional Freudian psychoanalysis. This assertion is time and culture bound, while her general theory probably is not. Therefore, a more general assertion is required: some kind of strong ideological justification for presumed gender differences will typically undergird a system of male homosociality.

Homosociality is neither a biologically rooted phenomenon, as some sociobiologists claim, nor simply repressed homosexuality. It is rooted in the fact that males possess more resources than females, which make women less useful and interesting to men and to other women alike. If women are to share men's world at all, they must emphasize what they feel men want most from them and other men are presumably unable or unwilling to provide: sexuality, motherhood, and service. The male homosocial world is thus self-sufficient and does not need deliberately to conspire to keep women segregated. Merely by ignoring women outside of these three contexts, "the male homosocial world relegates women to the sidelines of life" (1976:31).

The eclectic theories reviewed to this point have focused on general, societal level structures, and especially ideologies and normative systems. Virtually all feminist theories recognize the central importance of the family in sustaining the gender status quo. I turn now to two theories that specifically focus their attention on the institution of the family.

Colin Bell and Howard Newby (1976) called upon Max Weber's ideas concerning authority relationships in their theory of how men stabilize and maintain their dominant position within marital relationships. Their basic theme was that women offer deference to their husbands, a deference that is ultimately rooted in superior male power. **Deference** refers to "a traditionally-legitimated hierarchical relationship" (1976:155). That is, women do as men want primarily because they think they ought to. Power without deference is inherently unstable. It is therefore in the interests of those in superordinate positions, men in this case, to cultivate deference from subordinates (women). But why do women defer? Wives learn to defer to their husbands by being

> provided with a consistent and coherent set of ideas which interpret the dominance of their husbands in a manner that reinforces their legitimacy. Evaluative and factual statements must be made to elide — not only *do* men hold power but they *ought* to do so. Male interpretations must be taken as correct interpretations. (1976:159, emphasis in the original)

Bell and Newby called this **ideological hegemony** and suggested that it entails the definition of the deferential relationship as natural and immutable.

Bell and Newby argued that a vital element in producing marital deference is childhood sex-role socialization. Moreover, deference is most easily stabilized in relatively small, face-to-face social structures and small territorial units. The home epitomizes this. Thus, the encouragement of home-centeredness for wives serves to control women by enhancing deferential definitions of their role (1976:160).

Bell and Newby argued that deferential interaction consists of two elements which oppose one another: differentiation or hierarchy, and positively affective identification, such that super- and subordinates perceive the relationship as a cooperative partnership. These two elements are potentially contradictory, so superordinates (husbands) must also be prepared to prevent or resolve tensions with their wives in such a way as to maintain the deferential aspect of the relationship. This is rendered relatively easy because "tension-management will be most effective and complete when based upon face-to-face contact (as between husband and wife) and where the superordinate (male) interpretations of her situation are the only ones available" — as they often are to isolated housewives (1976:158). Positive inducements also help to maintain the deferential relationship; chief among these are gifts. Gift-giving by superordinates to subordinates prompts feelings of faithfulness and gratitude. Because deference is paid by wives to a person as well as to a role, husbands may express their traditional authority in untraditional ways if changing circumstances require it (e.g., his unemployment, her employment), yet maintain deference and authority.

Ultimately, underlying traditional authority is power and its naked use can be resorted to if the deferential relationship threatens to break down. The two forms of power available to husbands are "the power of the hand and the power of the purse"—coercive and economic power (1976:164). Nonetheless, especially physical coercion is an inherently unstable basis for interpersonal relationships, which can usually be stabilized only if the moral element of deference is present.

Bell and Newby concluded on a pessimistic note that the deferential relationship of marital partners appears very resistant to change. Moreover, it serves as a major inhibitor of the development among wives of a consciousness of their subordinate position (1976:166–7).

CURTIS

Like Bell and Newby, Richard Curtis (1986) approached the issue of the role of the family in perpetuating gender inequality using a Weberian perspective supplemented by Exchange theory. He began by noting that families redistribute the resources acquired from the larger society among their members. Such redistribution is a function of the family power structure, which, with substantial regularity, favors males over females (and adults over children). Curtis distinguished power from authority, arguing that although the two can vary independently, the latter often undergirds the former. Following Max Weber's conceptualization, power is defined in terms of the ability to affect the behavior of others despite their wishes. By contrast, authority entails the moral right of persons who occupy certain social positions to make decisions on behalf of others, a right that is acceded to by others. In addition to authority, male power over their wives often accrues from "control of resources, physical force, influence, manipulation of interests, strategic scheming, intimidation, and knowledge" (1986:171). Nonetheless, the most important source of power underlying patriarchy is authority. Moreover, relative to other sources of power, authority is superior because of its future orientation: it involves a stake in deciding issues that have not yet even been formulated (1986:172).

Male superiority in authority is rooted in their experience in authority systems outside the family. Male superiority also accrues from the traditional and widespread fact that economic resources, produced outside the family, are brought into it by men, giving them resource control. Thus, restriction to their own sphere within the family serves to deprive women of power even within that sphere, as well as in the broader society. Curtis asserted insightfully that inequality between the sexes is usually not based on the fact that women lack rights, but on the fact that their rights are apt to define women's sphere in a way that leaves men with more general access to power. The more extensive the male authority in a society, in fact, the more specific rights women are apt to have, and the less power in society those rights are likely to give them. (1986:173)

Looking more closely at power structures within families and how these affect the redistribution of resources garnered from the larger society, Curtis developed a social exchange model. He argued that social exchange must be distinguished from a very different kind of exchange: economic. Economic exchange is based on an enforceable agreement between the parties and relies upon trust in impersonal systems of enforcement. It specifies in detail what is to be traded for what, and it does so at the actual time of the transaction. By contrast, social exchange, which consists of gifts and favors, is more implicit; it is not rooted in explicit agreement. It relies on the debtor's good will at some time in the future. This type of exchange is rooted in trust of the individual. Social exchange sets up a diffuse debt for the recipient that can be called in at any later point. The result is that a person who has accumulated noneconomic (social) debts acquires interpersonal power (1986:176–7).

Social exchange, not economic exchange, is the primary basis of family relations and hence family power structures. Curtis argued: "The smoothest way to convert patriarchal authority into power is to store up debts for the future with lots of gifts to wife and children" (1986:177). Men can do this because their extrafamilial roles provide them income, social connections, and skills in the use of authority and power traditionally superior to those of their wives. The dependence that results from social exchange far surpasses that which results from contractual inequality: "The amount of debt incurred in noneconomic exchange, though unspecified, can be infinite in effect" (1986:179). It is not at all clear when such a debt has been discharged. Moreover, the resulting inequality between husbands and wives is concealed, both by the imprecision of social exchange and because what are essentially economic debts can be defined as coming under noneconomic rules of exchange. He gave as an example of this the fact that

> men can receive from their wives a market value of housework that is greater than their own incomes, yet the housework is only a portion of what the wife contributes in order to have a partial claim on that income. (1986:179)

In his conclusion, Curtis reiterated his thesis by noting that the family constitutes the place "where the 'harsh' rules of the marketplace are 'softened' by bonds of love and friendship," with the result that women might ask "with friends like these what need do I have for enemies?" (1986:181). Authority, economic, and other power resources generated in the larger society accrue disproportionately to men in a gender-stratified society. These advantages are easily converted into superior male power that affects the nature of social exchange within families to the disadvantage of women. Finally, Curtis suggested in passing that familial experiences affect the economic bargaining position of women in the labor force. This assertion closes the circle, suggesting the self-perpetuating nature of systems of gender inequality.

Besides the family, the other social institution that constitutes a nearly universal focus of attention for feminist theory is the economy. The next several theories examine how nondomestic work contributes to the maintenance of gender inequality, beginning with one which attempts to integrate the institutions of family and work in such an explanation.

COSER AND ROKOFF

Based primarily upon Robert Merton's discussion of status/roles, Rose Coser and Gerald Rokoff (1982; first published 1971) have analyzed the status/role obligations of men and women in contemporary American society, demonstrating how these have worked to sustain the gender status quo. Their analysis is undoubtedly applicable to industrialized societies generally. They began by asserting that the most salient roles in modern American society are those of family and work. The latter provides the means for general social status. They demonstrated how each sex is assigned a different priority in terms of these two role sets. They also explored the ramifications of this for the achievement of high-status work roles, given that the two sets are spatially and temporally separated.

The sharp separation of family and work roles makes possible the "operation of mechanisms that facilitate and . . . routinize status articulation, that is, the decision a person must make as to which of the role sets he or she will give priority" (1982:40). But this refers only to normal or unproblematic situations. Under emergency situations it becomes apparent that such status articulation mechanisms operate differently for men and women because of the different normative expectations that attach to each sex category. An emergency exists when the time and effort normally devoted to one role is upset by demands made by another role (e.g., when a family emergency intrudes on work time or work is taken home and intrudes on family time). For men, work roles are culturally defined as those that receive priority under situations of conflicting expectations, while for women, they are family roles. This means that in an emergency, women tend to disrupt the functioning of their work organization, men of their families. However, men's disruptions of familial functioning for work obligations are socially legitimated, making the resolution of conflicts relatively unproblematic. The issue, then, is how women's disruptions of work organizations are handled.

Coser and Rokoff argued that the anticipation of work-family conflicts for women creates social anxiety, which in turn prompts the creation of mechanisms to reduce such disruptions, specifically work disruptions. They discussed two such mechanisms. The first is that "women tend to limit their options by 'wanting to do what they have to do'." The second is for employers to restrict women's access to opportunities (1982:43).

In terms of the first mechanism, females are taught to define themselves in terms of their family and seek recognition vicariously through the prestige and accomplishments of their husbands. Work outside of the home is defined as secondary and supportive of the family, not as a career, unless the woman wishes to forgo a family altogether. Since there exists no clear, routinized way for women to work out conflicting claims from both sets of roles, women by and large choose to absent themselves from high-status occupations.

The second mechanism focuses not on women per se, but on the occupations that are most readily open to them. Coser and Rokoff argued that female-dominated occupations, unlike high prestige, male-dominated ones, assume that individuals are readily replaceable on the job (e.g., the institutionalization of substitute teaching). They made it clear that this assumption is not inherent in the nature of the work per se. The assumption flows from the organization's anticipation of high rates of absenteeism, the result of women responding to emergency family demands. They also argued that female-dominated occupations demand relatively little internal, psychological job commitment, as opposed to behavioral conformity to job requirements. The more prestigious occupations, however, all demand high levels of psychological commitment and are therefore filled by men. It is assumed by employers that the type of commitment men make to their occupations, women make to their families. Again, Coser and Rokoff were not arguing that it is the nature of the work that demands less commitment, only that female-dominated occupations are willing to accept less.

Finally, because of the assumption that family roles constitute women's first priority, a self-fulfilling prophecy functions. Based on that assumption, women are less likely to be trained, or if trained less likely to be hired for higher status occupational roles. In turn, women are less likely to seek such training or roles, and if they begin the process of doing so, they are more likely to drop out.

SEGMENTED LABOR MARKET

The recent research literature in sociology and economics contains a large number of mostly descriptive and empirical articles based on the Dual or

Segmented Labor Market approach, which implies a basic theory (see Sokoloff, 1981 and Chafetz, 1984:74–5 for brief reviews). This perspective argues that there is more than one labor market in advanced industrial societies, and that men and women are segregated into different markets (as are other minorities compared to white males). Typically, two such markets, termed the primary and the secondary, are depicted. Jobs in the primary are characterized by good wages, advancement opportunity, decent working conditions, substantial autonomy from close supervision and control, and relative job security. Because they are good jobs, employers usually have enough applicants that they can be selective. Those are the jobs (white) men fill. Secondary jobs have the opposite characteristics. Employers have fewer people from whom to select and the result is that women (and other minorities) are disproportionately found in these. This approach argues that the characteristics of the job shape worker attitudes and behaviors. Secondary sector workers tend to experience frequent job changes due both to job insecurity and to a search for better wages. In addition, they respond to the nature of their work by developing a lack of independence, confidence, achievement motivation, and commitment. These traits then serve to make them undesirable to employers of primary labor, with the result that secondary workers become trapped in that segment of the labor force (see Barron and Norris, 1976:50). The self-reinforcing cycle of inequality is thus explained.

What is less well explained in the Segmented Labor Market approach is why women disproportionately come to be employed in the secondary segment at the outset of their work lives. Typically, employer prejudice and stereotypes concerning the attributes of potential employees are mentioned as the major reasons. Barron and Norris (1976) provided a relatively complete statement of this explanation. They asserted:

> Given the limited information about potential job applicants normally available to recruiters, it may often be difficult for an employer to obtain direct evidence about the likely reliability and stability of a potential employee. Therefore use is frequently made of relatively visible . . . characteristics which are thought to correlate highly with these qualities. (1976:53)

They claimed that there are "five main attributes that may make a particular social group . . . a likely source of secondary workers: dispensability, clearly visible social difference, little interest in acquiring training, low economism and lack of solidarity" (1976:53). Women are highly dispensable, both because of high rates of voluntary turnover due to family responsibilities and because it is more socially acceptable to fire them than men. Obviously, women are visibly different from men. Women tend to seek and receive less job-related training because of social stereotypes that encourage them to believe that careers and marriage are antithetical. The authors argued that women are less concerned with economism (placing a high value on monetary rewards) because they perceive themselves as secondary earners in the family. Finally, women are much less involved in unions and therefore lack the level of worker solidarity characteristic of men. Barron and Norris claimed that these very traits, which are used by employers as a basis to bar women from primary labor market jobs, are exacerbated when women are placed in secondary labor market jobs.

A socialization perspective is often implicit in this structural theory of why women are handicapped in employment opportunities and income. Barron and Norris implied that, in addition to employer stereotypes, women in fact do not possess the same work-relevant characteristics as men at the outset of their employment history. The situation ostensibly arises from gender differentiated perceptions of the relative importance of family and employment role obligations, rooted in the socialization process. Socialization-based differences, combined with social stereotypes, lead women to jobs (in the secondary market) that magnify those very traits deemed undesirable by employers in the primary sector, thereby solidifying women's disadvantages throughout the life cycle.

Kanter

A major focus of the Segmented Labor Market theory is the assertion that jobs create worker characteristics, a perspective well developed by Rosabeth Kanter. She propounded a theory of the effects of three structural variables on the work behaviors of men and women in a series of papers, culminating in the award-winning book *Men and Women of the Corporation* (1977). Her central argument was that the variables—opportunities, power, and relative numbers—affect people within a bureaucratic organization in a similar manner, regardless of the personal attributes they initially bring to the job. The extent to which men and women are found in positions that elicit negative effects differs—women are much more likely to suffer from blocked opportunities, powerlessness, and numerical scarcity (tokenism). The reactions to such situations include the reinforcement of negative stereotypes about women and a decline in their job commitment, aspirations, and opportunities for future advancement. In short, organizational functioning reinforces the very disadvantages that women suffer because of their gender before and upon entry into an organization. Kanter's theory was embedded in a study of one corporate bureaucracy. Nonetheless, it should be widely applicable to other corporations and other types of bureaucracies. Because so many people work for bureaucratic organizations in modern industrial societies, the ramifications of her argument for the maintenance of general, societal-level gender inequality are substantial.

Kanter depicted the central organizational value in terms of upward career mobility: advancement over time within a strongly hierarchical system. By their very nature, hierarchies narrow in a roughly pyramidal fashion, so that most people will eventually find themselves in a position from which no further vertical movement is possible. This constitutes **blocked mobility**. Clerical and secretarial workers in particular, virtually all of whom are women and who often comprise the vast majority of women employed by an organization, are apt to find themselves in positions of blocked opportunity. Career ladders for these jobs are typically short and quickly reach a dead-end (1977:chapter 4 and 136). Kanter postulated that when workers perceive an opportunity to advance, their aspirations, work commitment, and sense of organizational responsibility are all enhanced. In turn, such traits enhance their promotability. When faced with blocked opportunity, however, people typically respond by lowering their aspirations to conform to reality; by reducing their commitment to and interest in the organization and work in general; by withdrawing from responsibility; by increasing their interest in and commitment to peers and sociability, including the development of an anti-success, peer-solidarity ethic; by seeking recognition from outsiders, junior personnel, or subordinates rather than peers and superiors; and by engaging in conservative resistance such as resisting innovation, being chronically critical, playing it safe, and refusing to take risks. In turn, such attitudes and behaviors further reduce any opportunities for advancement that may have arisen (1977:chapter 6).

Kanter defined power as "the ability to get things done, to mobilize resources, to get and use whatever it is that a person needs for the goals he or she is attempting to meet" (1977:166). Armed with power, people are able to achieve more power. When people are known to be able to achieve goals, others support them and follow their leadership, thereby further enhancing their power and effectiveness. People want a powerful boss because such a superior expedites the upward mobility of her or his subordinates. One may have a position of ostensible responsibility and authority, yet lack power, as Kanter defined it. People who are responsible for supervising others yet lack power will tend to engage in ineffective and unpopular forms of leadership. These include coercive and controlling behavior, too close supervision of subordinates, rigid and narrow conformity to rules and formalities, and territorial protectiveness (1977:189–95). They therefore provoke resistance, which further reduces their power and effectiveness, resulting in a vicious cycle.

Women especially, argued Kanter, are caught in this cycle of powerlessness, resulting in or reinforcing a stereotype of women managers that closely resembles the characteristics of powerless leaders generally. In turn, that stereotype leads people to prefer men as leaders, because they equate maleness with power (1977:197–205). Women leaders are typically found encapsulated in organizationally powerless positions (e.g., secretarial and clerical supervisors) with no further mobility prospects. Placed outside of the mainstream of the organization, they lack alliances with powerful managers. In these ways, they are rendered yet more powerless.

The third structural variable discussed by Kanter, and the most important in terms of feminist theory, is **relative numbers**, and specifically the **token** position in which women in higher status positions typically find themselves (1977:chapter 8). Tokens are defined as a proportional representation of 15 percent or less of one category of people (women), compared to the 85 percent or more dominants from another category (men) as peers in a particular work group. The master feature of tokens is their conspicuousness; no matter what they do, they are highly visible. In addition, dominants see tokens as different from and contrasting with themselves — indeed they typically exaggerate the differences — again no matter what the tokens do. Dominants also assimilate tokens into their stereotype of the token's category (femaleness in this case), often distorting their perceptions of individual women in order to do so. Kanter cited as the results of these three reactions:

> Visibility tends to create *performance pressures* on the token. Contrast leads to heightening of *dominant culture boundaries*, including isolation of the token. And assimilation results in the token's *role encapsulation*. (1977:212, emphases in the original)

While tokens are more conspicuous than others, their job performance is often ignored, as the perceptions of dominants are focused on the token's master status — her femaleness. Nonetheless, if a token woman performs poorly, it is taken as proof that women are not equipped to do the job properly. If she does well, she risks retaliation from dominants who may suffer by comparison. Such retaliation, in turn, will typically impede her ability to effectively perform her job.

Tokens' responses to their situation and the pressures it induces are potentially several. None serve to enhance their careers in the long run; several exact high psychic costs; and some serve to re-create difficulties for other women. They can respond to performance pressures in three ways: (1) overachieve, ignore peers, and pay the price of their resentment; (2) accept their notoriety and difference and trade on it, which often entails actively working to keep other women out, thereby reinforcing tokenism; or (3) try to become invisible by keeping a low profile, which allows others to take credit for their work (1977:219–21). They have two alternatives in responding to cultural boundary heightening by dominants: they can accept isolation, thereby being excluded from important communication, knowledge, and opportunities; or they can try to prove their loyalty by turning against other women.

Role encapsulation refers to the effect of stereotyped expectations by dominants. Tokens may find themselves occupying a formal position reserved specifically for women, which may have a fancy title but probably no power, and which will be a dead-end job. Tokens also find that dominants cast them into one of several informal roles: mother, seductress, pet, or iron maiden. Each of these is fraught with its own difficulties, which Kanter described in some detail (1977:233–6). She concluded:

> It . . . [is] often easier to accept stereotyped roles than to fight them, even if their acceptance . . . [means] limiting the token's range of expressions or demonstrations of task competence, because they . . . [offer] a comfortable and certain position. The personal consequence for tokens . . . [is] a measure of self-distortion. (1977:236).

In accepting role encapsulation, dominants' stereotypes are reinforced, limiting the future possibilities for women in general. In short, regardless of how individual token women choose to respond to the pressures emanating from their scarcity, their responses will typically reinforce stereotypes and function to perpetuate tokenism itself. Their responses also reduce tokens' own work opportunities and create psychic discomfort for them.

Blocked opportunity, powerlessness, and tokenism are common problems for women in the formal organizations that dominate modern industrial societies such as our own. Women in organizations react like others confronting the same problems; however, for women their responses ultimately serve to reinforce the very system of gender inequality that disproportionately places them in such situations in the first place. Unlike most of the theories discussed already or later in this chapter, Kanter's theory does not treat gender differences as real. Men and women do not have different personalities, skills, and values rooted in differential socialization; rather, women react the same way as men when they share the same structural positions and opportunities. It is the **differential placement** of women that **produces** the work-related behaviors and attitudes that are typically stereotyped as basic feminine traits.

Meeker and Weitzel-O'Neill

One final, brief structural theory also has ramifications for the organizational level of analysis. Social psychologists Barbara Meeker and Patricia Weitzel-O'Neill (1985; see also Lockheed, 1985) developed a theory of gender roles and behavior in task-oriented small groups. While the theory has a very specific and narrow focus, I believe that it also has substantial implications for understanding how systems of gender inequality perpetuate themselves. They based their approach on two general theories: Performance Expectation and Status Consistency. They began with an assumption of male status superiority. From Performance Expectancy theory they were then able to deduce that in group situations, males, for whom there are higher performance expectations based on their superior status,

> will receive and take more opportunities to make task contributions, will have more influence and more prestige, and will receive more expressions of agreement and approval [than females] . . . . (1985:387)

Status Consistency theory lends several further insights. For people with high status external to the group, but not those with low external status, raising their own status relative to that of others in the group is considered legitimate. Therefore, again assuming preexisting male superiority in status, men are expected to act in a manner that raises their status. Such acts will be neither expected nor accepted from women (1985:389). In short, preexisting inequities between the sexes create expectations which, at the face-to-face level of small group interaction, serve to reinforce male advantage.

SUMMARY

In the introduction to this chapter, two specifically macrolevel issues and one issue bridging the micro- and macrolevels were enumerated. The bridging issue concerned how real, average differences between the sexes, which presumably arise from early socialization, become relevant to sustaining a system of gender inequality. The theories discussed in this section have had relatively little to say about this issue. Holter included psychological functioning as one of a number of variables in her book. She centered her later attention more clearly on this. However, she did not go into detail about *how* the presumably different personalities of males and females become translated into unequal opportunities. Fox gave a more detailed explanation of how, by internalizing the injunction to be ladylike, females disadvantage themselves. Likewise, Dual Labor Market theorists Barron and Norris suggested, as a minor component of their explanation, that because of differential socialization, men and women bring different traits to the labor force initially, with men possessing those that are more highly valued by employers. The Dual Labor Market theory, and especially Kanter's, however, emphasized the opposite phenomenon: that differential placement of men and women in employment settings *creates* gender differentiated traits at the individual level, which then further handicap women in pursuit of labor market opportunities.

One of the two macrolevel issues raised in the introduction to this chapter concerned cultural beliefs about gender differences, and how, regardless of their veracity, they help to sustain systems of gender stratification. Most of the theories discussed in this section have as a central focus one or both of two variables relevant to this issue. On the one hand, there is the phenomenon of ideological systems that legitimate inequality between the sexes, an emphasis we have already encountered in the Marxist-feminist approach. Discussions of ideology ranged from legitimation of male dominance within the family (e.g., Bell and Newby) to more general treatments of its role in legitimating a broad system of gender stratification (e.g., Chafetz, Holter, Lipman-Blumen). Ideology functions to sustain a system by convincing the disadvantaged, as well as the advantaged, of the rightness of that system. On the other hand, there is a focus on gender norms. Such norms involve social expectations of behavior which are sex linked, and which affect both the opportunities made available to women and the choices made by women (e.g., Holter, Fox, Chafetz, Meeker and Weitzel-O'Neill, Bell and Newby, Coser and Rokoff, Barron and Norris). Gender norms were seen as important in structuring the actual social roles women and men play, functioning to support gender inequality by dissuading or preventing women from engaging in those roles that afford high levels of prestige, wealth, and power. The norms themselves may be viewed as legitimated by an overarching ideology, which serves to convince both sexes of the propriety of the status quo.

The second macroissue raised at the outset of the chapter concerned structural elements other than cultural definitions, which function to sustain a system of male advantage. Guttentag and Secord's theory stressed the importance of the demographic variable sex ratio in understanding how gender inequality is exacerbated. The structural variable that most often played a central theoretical role is the resource advantage which accrues to males primarily from their role in the economy. This constituted an important component of several theories (e.g., Lipman-Blumen, Bell and Newby, Curtis, Chafetz). Resource advantage is seen as constituting the major basis for power inequities, which in turn are used to reinforce an opportunity structure and set of cultural expectations that advantage males. This is also an important, in fact a central, component of Marxist-feminist analysis. Several theories also include male coercive power, but each tends to consider this of minor importance (Holter, Bell and Newby, Curtis).

In the remainder of this chapter attention will be focused on the microlevel of direct, interpersonal interaction — especially in childhood socialization and spousal interaction. Social norms, ideologies, and power are not irrelevant to, or absent from, these theories; however, where they are the focal points of theories reviewed up to this point, they now become background issues for most of the theories reviewed in the rest of the chapter.

FEMINIST NEO-FREUDIAN THEORIES

CHODOROW

As mentioned in the last chapter, Chodorow's feminist revision of Psychoanalytic theory (1978) is best suited for explaining how systems of gender inequality are maintained. The very use of the term reproduction in the title of her book conveyed this orientation. At the most general level, the answer she provided for this issue is that because women do the vast amount of the early childrearing, they rear girls, but not boys, who want to do likewise. They produce boys who are fearful of women yet insist on the superiority of their sex and male dominance. In reproducing these psychic predispositions, they re-create the division of labor by which women mother and men turn their attentions to the public world. In turn, this division of labor is the root of systems of gender inequality, and it functions to perpetuate intergenerationally the psychodynamics of the entire process.

Chodorow's explanation of the processes for each sex that lead to such systems of gender inequality will be discussed now. It is important to understand that the dynamics described by Chodorow occur in contemporary families in which women are overwhelmingly responsible for childcare. They are not inherent in the species or in any way necessary. Rather they are a function of current socioeconomic arrangements and childrearing practices of the recent past.

Because of their extreme dependency, during infancy both boys and girls are closely attached to their mothers (primary caretakers) and fail to perceive themselves as differentiated from them. This sense of oneness that infants experience with their primary caretaker is the basis for the human capacity to relate to and love others later in life. However, mothers react to their infants and toddlers differently depending on the child's sex. After infancy, children must begin to learn to separate from their mothers and develop a sense of themselves as separate people: a sense of independence. Chodorow posited (1978:especially chapter 6) that because they share the same sex, mothers experience a sense of oneness and continuity with their daughters; but they experience more of a sense, often sexualized, of otherness in relationship to their sons. The result is that mothers tend to delay the process of separation and individuation in their daughters, while stressing it in their sons. This describes the situation for children in their preoedipal period, which is longer for girls than boys because of the mother's differential responses.

During the oedipal stage, these early differences are further elaborated, resulting in very different relational capacities and needs in the two sexes. The primary task of this stage is the development of a heterosexual orientation and this, in turn, involves identification with the same-sex parent.

Chodorow argued that not only do girls enter this stage later, but that they never relinquish the preoedipal relationship with their mothers as completely as do boys. Thus, females remain throughout life "preoccupied with issues of symbiosis and primary love without sense of the other person's separateness" (1978:115). It is this preoccupation that ultimately leads females (but not males) to reproduce mothering.

Chodorow noted that fathers usually sex-type their children along traditional gender-role lines more consciously than do mothers. The father thus actively encourages his daughter's flirtatiousness towards himself. At the same time, the length and intensity of the daughter's preoedipal attachment to her mother leads the daughter to reject her mother and turn to her father in her search for independence. Chodorow saw the girl's oedipal stage as at least as much a rejection of dependence on her mother as it is a positive orientation towards her father (1978:123-6). But the father is relatively absent in the girl's life. He is therefore not likely to engender the depth of love that the primary caretaker does. Thus, girls are likely to maintain both parents as love objects, although with considerable ambiguity toward the mother. The result is that while the girl will usually develop heterosexually, she creates a triangle by never relinquishing her mother as a love object, and simply adding her father as a love object on to her attachment to her mother.

The male oedipal experience is quite different. Chodorow argued that the boy's repression of his maternal attachment seems to be more complete than a girl's. This is in part because the boy's oedipal love for his mother is more threatening to his sense of independence and his sense of himself as a masculine person. In part also it is a function of the fact that the normally sexualized mother-son bond is more threatening to the husband/father than the mother-daughter relationship, and causes the father to resent his son. In short, a boy is more motivated to give up his attachment to his mother than a girl is. But also, a girl is less motivated to give up her oedipal attraction to her father than a boy is to relinquish his oedipal attraction to his mother. In relinquishing his oedipal mother-attachment and identifying with his father, the boy gains both his heterosexuality and a stronger superego than his sister. He does not, however, move into the kind of emotional triangle with both parents that she does. Indeed, given the relative absence of fathers, boys tend to develop their sense of masculine identity in heavily negative terms as that which is not feminine. Boys also learn masculinity as an abstraction rather than through close personal identification with their fathers.

Chodorow concluded that the oedipal stage has different meanings for girls and boys. For boys, gender identification is the central issue. For girls, it is psychosexual development. Since both are originally involved with a female love object (their mother), girls gain a heterosexual orientation from the oedipal stage. For boys "the major goal is the achievement of personal masculine identification . . . and sense of secure masculine self, achieved through superego formation and disparagement of women" (1978:165). The two sexes also come out of this stage with different forms of relational potential, which was for Chodorow the most important result:

> . . . a girl continues to experience herself as involved in issues of merging and separation, and in an attachment characterized by primary identification and the fusion of identification and object choice. . . . A boy has engaged, and been required to engage in a more emphatic individuation and a more defensive firming of experienced ego boundaries. (1978:166–7)

There is thus a greater psychological basis for empathy in girls than boys. Moreover, since they did not repress their preoedipal attachment so totally, females are less threatened than males by returning to these modes later in life. For females, while relationships are central to their lives, men tend to remain emotionally secondary to them. For males, denial of connectedness and isolation of affect, along with a more rigid and punitive superego, result from the oedipal process (1978:169). In short, females spend their lives substantially more preoccupied with relational issues than do males, for whom denial of connectedness is equivalent to denial of femininity. In turn, these psychic differences prepare boys for participation in nonrelational spheres of life, such as economic and other public roles, and girls for relational spheres, especially the domestic sphere and maternal role. Women seek to reproduce the sense of connectedness they experienced with their mothers by having children, especially since their husbands are likely to find it difficult and threatening to meet their wives' emotional needs (1978:199).

In this way the division of labor by gender is reproduced, along with the system of inequality that it undergirds. Indeed,

> given that masculinity is so elusive, it becomes important for masculine identity that certain social activities are defined as masculine and superior, and that women are believed unable to do many of the things defined as socially important. . . . A boy's contempt serves to free him not only from his mother but also from the femininity within himself [and] . . . therefore . . . is generalized to all women. (1978:182)

But if women's mothering produces misogyny and a sense of superiority in males, it also produces love. This results in the male tendency to glorify and adore women. Such ambivalence leads men to "search for nonthreatening, undemanding, dependent, even infantile women" (1978:185). The structure of parenting thus creates ideological and psychological orientations towards male dominance.

KITTAY

In the last chapter I treated Kittay's theory of womb envy (1983) as a statement of cause, while Chodorow's similar theory has been treated primarily as an analysis of how systems of gender inequality are maintained. This is largely because Chodorow explicitly recognized variability in the extent of such inequality, while Kittay implied that female subordination is a constant. In the former case, there was recognition that societal differences in parental behavior, specifically paternal involvement, have existed and are rooted in varying degrees of gender stratification. In the latter case, a constant (womb envy) was seen as creating and maintaining another constant (female subordination). However, I believe that Kittay's approach, like Chodorow's, is in fact best viewed as an explanation of how female subordination is reproduced, once in existence. As in Chodorow's case, Kittay assumed that mothers are the primary caretakers of infants and that fathers are involved little if at all in the process. This division of labor, however, probably manifests a preexisting sexual inequality, thus making the causal argument circular. Kittay suggested in her conclusions (discussed in chapter 5 of this book), that womb envy, and the resultant subordination of women, would not occur were fathers more fully integrated into the early caretaking of their children. However, because of womb envy, men are likely to devalue child-rearing and therefore refrain from nurturing youngsters. In turn, this produces sons who suffer womb envy, thus continuously reinforcing the gender stratification system.

RUBIN

Rubin's revision of Lévi-Strauss's theory, which argued that the exchange of women as marriage partners stands at the root of gender inequality, was discussed in chapter 2. In order for such an exchange to occur, people must learn culturally appropriate definitions of gender and heterosexuality, and to focus on nonkin as potential mates. Rubin turned to Freud in order to understand how these conventions are learned by children, thus permitting the perpetuation of the system.

Rubin argued that it is primarily in the process of resolving the oedipal crisis that children develop these socially appropriate components of personality. It is during this process that

> children discover the differences between the sexes, and that each child must become one or the other gender. They also discover the incest taboo . . . [and that] the mother is unavailable to either child because she "belongs" to the father. Lastly, they discover that the

two genders do not have the same sexual "rights" or futures. (1975:193).

She then offered a revised version of the Freudian thesis concerning the male oedipal crisis and its resolution. She traced how the boy experiences castration anxiety, which for Rubin is couched as the loss of the *culturally* valued phallus as a symbol of superiority; and how he renounces his incestuous desires for his mother, and affirms the relationships which, upon maturity, will give him a woman of his own. In short, said Rubin, "the boy exchanges his mother for the phallus, the symbolic token which can later be exchanged for a woman"—if only he is patient (1975:193).

The girl's case is more complex because it entails the discovery of unpleasant information about the gender to which she is being assigned. For her brother, the taboo is on his mother; for her, it is on all women. She finds out that women can only properly be loved by someone with a phallus, and since she lacks that, she has no right to love her mother. This conclusion is not reached, according to Rubin, because of any sexual understanding of the role of the penis. Rather,

> the hierarchical arrangement of the male and female genitals is a result of the . . . rule of obligatory heterosexuality and the relegation of women (those without phallus . . .) to men (those with the phallus). (1975:194)

So the girl turns away from her mother in anger and disappointment that her mother didn't give her that symbol of cultural superiority, a phallus. In turning to her father, she cannot, like her brother, receive a phallus. Rather, she "accedes to the place of a woman in a phallus exchange network" and accepts intercourse or a child as a substitute—a gift from a man (1975:195). In this way, the female becomes subordinated and domesticated.

Rubin summarized the relationship between the two parts of her theory, that derived from Lévi-Strauss and that from Freudian analysis:

> Kinship systems require a division of the sexes. The Oepidal phase divides the sexes. Kinship systems include sets of rules governing sexuality. The Oedipal crisis is the assimilation of these rules and taboos. Compulsory heterosexuality is the product of kinship. The Oedipal phase constitutes heterosexual desire. Kinship rests on a radical difference between the rights of men and women. The Oedipal complex confers male rights upon the boy, and forces the girl to accommodate herself to her lesser rights. (1975:198)

SOCIALIZATION THEORIES

The neo-Freudian theories just examined root the intergenerational transmission of the gender system in early childhood experiences and responses. The Socialization theories do likewise. For the neo-Freudians, the process is unconscious for both the children and adults. It results from the very fundamental fact that women do most, if not virtually all, of the caretaking in infancy and early childhood. For them, the reproduction of gender is a very deep process. The Socialization theorists are more concerned with the manner in which parents, peers, and environmental factors *teach* gender to children. For them, gender is reproduced, not as an automatic result of mothering, but as the outcome of a variety of specific types of learning experiences normally experienced by growing children.

Because of this emphasis, the literature on gender socialization, though vast, is largely descriptive and empirical. Most of it concentrates on detailing the specifics of how contemporary American children are taught gender by parents, peers, media, schools, toys, and so on. In the following pages I have selected for focus a few publications that are oriented somewhat more broadly to the process of gender socialization rather than to the detailed particulars that are highly time and space bound.

CAHILL

The Symbolic Interaction perspective on gender socialization is represented by the work of Spencer Cahill (1983). His theory pertained to the acquisition of gender identity and socially normative gender behavior, which is not an explicit theory of the maintenance of systems of gender inequality. Nonetheless, the intergenerational transmission of gender-based behaviors and self-concepts, within an existing system of inequality, must certainly be considered a mechanism — perhaps a major one — that supports the status quo.

Cahill began by asserting that it is the social reaction to biological sex differences that makes such differences meaningful, not the differences themselves. The first such reaction is the sex labeling of infants at birth. The labels affect parental behavioral responses and conceptions of their child, and in this way constitute one of the most influential factors in a child's early social interactional experience. Because others respond to the infant on the basis of sex, sex becomes salient to the child's emerging sense of self. As the child matures, he or she becomes more competent in labeling both self and others in terms of sex. This then enables the child to identify with membership in one or the other category. Thus, gender identity emerges simultaneously with linguistic competence in the use of gender labels. The child also comes to associate a self-label with certain responses to his or her self. In short,

the two critical factors in the formation of gender identity . . . seem to be others' differential patterns of responsiveness to
male and female infants and others' associated use of sex-designating
verbal labels. Male and female infants' different social experience
leads to sex differences in both early conceptions of self and in overt
behavior. . . . The child learns that the way he or she is responded
to, behaves, and feels is due to sex-category membership. (1983:6)

Cahill argued that gender identity provides children with a mechanism to locate themselves in relation to others. Children seek to confirm this identity
in social interaction, and thus use it as a basic organizer of experience. In actively seeking out gender-identity-confirming responses from others, children learn which behaviors elicit a response, and thus learn the gender ideals
or norms of the social group.

Children do not, however, employ trial-and-error in figuring out which
behaviors will elicit gender-confirming response. A major mechanism they
employ is same-sex models, although this need not be a parent. It can include,
in addition to other people, idealized gender models in children's books, television, and so on. Nor is modeling the only source of information about gender ideals available in the child's environment. Cahill cited room decor and
toys as examples of additional sources. The child's active search for gender
confirmation is typically conducted within an environment constructed in
conformity with the gender norms of his or her social group, and it is well
stocked with same-sex adult models.

In addition to parents and other adults, peer interactions and play constitute important sources of gender confirmation. Cahill stated:

In play children construct social worlds around sexual classification
and rehearse their performance of gender-specific behaviors. Although adults set the gender development process in motion, children refine and develop their understanding and performance of
gender among peers. (1983:10)

Moreover, children learn that the more their sex labeling of activities cor-
responds to adult notions of gender appropriateness, the more the adults support them. "In short, children re-create the sexual division of social activities
in their exclusive social worlds" (1983:10). In play, children develop gender
competence and also learn to anticipate the behavior of the other gender.
They learn to script cross-sex interactions in much the same way they will
be required to do so later in life.

Cahill concluded by reiterating that the interactionist perspective recognizes that the gender expectations and norms developed by children generally correspond to those of adults in their social groups. Adults guide children's gender development in subtle and indirect ways, but they learn to

perform gender specific behaviors, and also to be normally sexed, primarily among peers. Obviously, to the extent that a child's parents and those of the child's peers express traditional conceptions of gender, from this theoretical perspective the child will develop a traditional notion of her or his own gendered self and traditional expectations of gendered behavior by others.

LEVER

The importance of play for gender socialization was also stressed by Janet Lever (1976), who drew in part on the ideas of George Herbert Mead. She theorized that children's play constitutes an activity of socialization, the products of which are specific role skills. Girls and boys are usually taught and encouraged to play in very different ways, both by the adults with whom they are in contact and by other children. As a result, they achieve very different role skills.

> Specifically . . . boys' games . . . help prepare their players for successful performance in a wide variety of work settings in modern society. In contrast, girls' games . . . help prepare their players for the private sphere of the home and their future roles as wives and mothers. (1976:484)

What, exactly, do boys' games teach, compared to those typical for girls? The former

> further independence training, encourage the development of organizational skills necessary to coordinate the activities of a numerous and diverse group of people, and offer experience in rule-bounded events and adjudication of disputes. (1976:484)

Boys also learn through play how to deal with interpersonal competition and not take it personally. Girls, on the other hand, develop delicate socioemotional skills in their play, which is relatively cooperative and free of competition, structure, and rules. Their play takes place in settings of only a few peers and especially in dyads. Using the language of Mead, Lever concluded that boys are learning to take the role of the generalized other, girls the role of the particular other in their play. Thus, Lever concluded that children's play contributes to the perpetuation of differential abilities between the sexes, which in turn reinforce traditional gender roles.

CONSTANTINOPLE

Psychologist Anne Constantinople (1979) combined elements of Social Learning and Cognitive Developmental theories in an attempt to understand how people acquire their sex role identity in early childhood. Her focus was upon gender roles as a set of rules children learn in order to control their own behavior. Given a level of cognitive development determined by age, the child uses information provided by the environment to construct rules, in an effort to avoid negative responses and receive positive ones. Therefore, sex roles become heavily tinged with an emotional component, leading to anxiety in later life when rules associated with them are broken. Children have an innate capacity to generalize, discriminate, and form categories. Their environment provides a set of specific sex-related cues, often quite subtle, that lead children to apply that capacity to gender. In order to do so, a child must have matured cognitively to the point where a labeling process can aid in disembedding sex-related stimuli from all other types in the environment. The initial core is provided by the sex-specific terminology employed ubiquitously by parents and others (e.g., boy, girl, man, woman, mommy, daddy). In short, language acquisition and sex-role acquisition go hand in hand. The labels help children to organize the knowledge gained from

> observational learning and direct tutelage. . . . Positive and negative reinforcement . . . serve both to focus the child's attention on relevant stimuli and to endow sex-role related behaviors with positive and negative affect. (1979:128)

Constantinople assumed that children need cognitive structure. Even very subtle differences in the reinforcement of the two sexes by parents, siblings, peers, and others increase the child's search for rules to distinguish the sexes and to aid in analyzing new situations for their gender-related content.

Lewis and Weinraub

Lewis and Weinraub (1979) also developed a cognitive theory of early sex-role development that emphasized the infant's and young child's active construction, rather than passive receipt, of gender conceptions. They began by asserting that infants acquire knowledge of themselves at the same time as they acquire knowledge of others. Part and parcel of that is the early acquisition of a basic understanding that there are two gender categories. Surrounded by pervasive cues that there are two sexes, the infant first constructs crude categories, later more refined ones, into which to place others as well as self. The meaning of these gender categories is supplied by the culture, but the impetus to construct them appears in this theory to be universal. Finally, children strive to act in a manner that is similar to that of others who are like themselves, and one major way of categorizing likeness is gender similarity. "In this way, the self actively and creatively develops culturally designated sex-role behavior" (1979:149).

In a brief essay, Rebecca, Hefner, and Oleshansky (1976) outlined a three-stage model of sex-role socialization, arguing that in our society most people never progress beyond the second stage. The result of this, in turn, is the continued existence of sharp gender differentiation and inequality.

Stage I was referred to as **undifferentiated sex roles**. The very young child at this stage is unaware of culturally imposed restrictions on behavior according to biological sex. They argued that one of the first value-laden distinctions children learn is the big-small polarity. Soon they come to associate bigness with both power and maleness. Simultaneously, they learn that they and all others belong to only one of two gender categories, each associated with its own set of appropriate and valued behaviors. At this point they enter stage II, **polarized sex roles**. During this stage socialization techniques are used by parents, schools, and society in general to assure the adoption of conventional perceptions and behaviors. Children come to actively accept their own conventional role and equally actively reject the other. The authors argued that this learning is functional and desirable because children use the organizing technique of polarities in order to make sense of an inherently indivisible world. However, strict adherence to this dichotomized conception of gender is not reserved for children; it is expected of adults throughout their lives, and this produces (more accurately, reproduces) gender inequality (1976:95).

Rebecca, Hefner, and Oleshansky argued that a third stage is possible, in fact desirable, although only a few individuals currently manage to achieve it. They call stage III **sex role transcendence**. At this stage, people are flexible, using those traits of personality and behavior most suitable to any given situation in which they find themselves. For such people, assigned gender has become irrelevant to decision-making. The third stage is possible because in the process of learning their own sex role in stage II, people learn the components of both roles. Those socially defined as belonging to the other sex typically remain latent because of social pressure, but they are available to be called up. However, in their conclusion the authors not only assert that there is virtually no support for a shift from levels II to III, they offer no concrete suggestions as to how such change could be brought about.

Coser

A variety of different theoretical perspectives examined earlier converged on one fundamental point: women's social disadvantages relative to men are heavily rooted in their domestic role, the playing of which helps to maintain existing gender inequities. In a recent paper, Rose Laub Coser (1986) theorized about the reasons why females tend to develop their cognitive abilities for abstraction less than men and instead orient themselves to the practical affairs of daily life. She postulated that as a result, women are not only at a competitive disadvantage in seeking high status jobs, but are more oriented toward assuming the domestic role.

Coser began by asserting that cognitive development is facilitated and enhanced by interactions with people occupying highly diverse roles and by occupying increasingly diverse roles oneself. Girls, as children, and especially as adolescents, have fewer of both kinds of experiences than do boys because of gender-linked cultural expectations. She posited that role relationships in the family are quite simple relative to those in the public sphere. The family is restricted not only socially, but also physically. Life within the family focuses on practical, everyday matters. The more a child is tied to the social world of the family and the physical site of the household, the less mental distance the child acquires. On the other hand, the more a child experiences mental distance, the more the child develops abilities to engage in abstract thinking. Girls are both socially and physically tied to the family and household more than are boys, in large measure as preparation for the later assumption of the domestic role. Relational systems that are weaker but more complex than the strong and simple familial ones offer opportunities for reflection, and therefore for the development of abstract thought. Girls, who are tied to the family, prepare for the simplicity of family relationships in later life.

The substance of Coser's argument is that because parents anticipate that their daughters will grow up to be homemakers functioning primarily in the domestic sphere, they constrain their physical mobility and social interactions more than for boys. In turn, such restrictions limit cognitive development, ultimately creating women who are relatively unfit to function outside the domestic sphere.

STATUS ATTAINMENT AND HUMAN CAPITAL THEORIES

One variant of the socialization perspective can be found in the numerous comparative studies of women and men in the labor force, done by economists and sociologists, that fall within the Status Attainment or Human Capital theoretical perspective (see Sokoloff, 1981 for a brief discussion). This research tradition, which has no one clear theoretical representative, argues that the reason women fail to achieve equity with men in the work force is that they bring to the labor market lesser amounts of those personal characteristics that make for high worker productivity (e.g., education, job-related training, and experience). They thus lose out in competition with men. In turn, women are said to be deficient in valued work-related traits, or **human capital**, because of their gender socialization, which shaped their aspirations, attitudes, and values toward education, work, and the family. Thus, gender-differentiated socialization functions to reproduce inequality by failing to arm females with the personal characteristics needed to successfully compete with men in the labor market.

HORNER

Psychologist Mattina Horner (1972) went even further in her much researched, much debated theory, which attributed to women a **fear of success**, arising from gender socialization. To the extent that females develop a psychological motive to avoid success, especially in situations of competition with men, a system of gender inequality is strongly reinforced (see Sutherland and Veroff, 1985, for a review of this literature).

SATTEL

If girls are socialized to traits conducive to domesticity, and antithetical to achievement, what is it that boys are supposedly socialized for? In a brief analysis of male emotional inexpressiveness, Sattel (1976) argued that this characteristic of masculinity is a potent tool that men use to achieve, consolidate, and maintain power in interpersonal interactions. Males use silence and inexpression to manipulate and control situations, both with women and other men, although most of his analysis focused on male-female interactions. Sattel argued that to be effective, power wielders must guard against emotional involvement with the consequences of their decisions. They must be able to show that their decisions are fair, efficient, rational, that is, nonemotional. Only then can they convince others of the rightness of their actions. Because it is assumed that males will be the decision makers and power wielders, boys are specifically socialized by parents and others to control and suppress the expression of emotion. In this way, males are armed with a technique that enables them to maintain the superior power of their sex.

SUMMARY

In this section, as in the last, the theories have focused on how children come to take on the preexisting identities, behaviors, personalities, and other traits socially defined as appropriate to their sex — on how they became gendered. Both the neo-Freudian and Socialization approaches assume that, among adults, gender differences are real. Each seeks to understand the processes by which that reality is produced, differing mostly in this aspect of their theories. Both suggest that in producing properly gendered females and males, the society is reproducing the division of labor which undergirds a system of gender inequality. Further, they each grant to parents a central role in this process.

Turning specifically to the gender socialization theories, the infant and child are seen as immersed in a social and linguistic world which is constantly sending gender signals. The child actively responds to these and in so doing develops an awareness of the existence of two genders; identifies the self as one of these; incorporates that gender as a fundamental component of her or his self-concept; and takes on those attributes of behavior, intellect, and personality socially defined as appropriate to that gender. The child is strongly supported and encouraged to undergo this process, and dissuaded from assuming attributes assigned to the other gender, chiefly by the responses of parents and peers. Among females this process is said to reproduce an orientation toward domesticity, and a lack, or insufficiency of those attributes required for success in the nondomestic, especially economic realm. For males, the result is essentially posited as the opposite. In turn, the Socialization theories at least implicitly assume that these gendered traits of personality, intellect, and behavior are quite stable over a lifetime, thereby fundamentally affecting adult role preference, selection, and performance.

EVERYDAY LIFE APPROACHES

The theories in this section focus on one or more of several interrelated issues: how, in everyday interactions with one another, men and women create a sense of gender for self and partner; how routine behavior is gendered; and how inequality is fostered during the process.

KESSLER AND MCKENNA

In their Ethnomethodological treatment of gender, Suzanne Kessler and Wendy McKenna (1978) did not explicitly address any of the four issues around which this book is organized. They explored in depth the issue of **gender attribution**, which is logically prior to, and thus constitutes the basis of, the maintenance and reproduction of gender systems. They examined the *process* by which people attribute gender to self and others — how in our society (but not all societies), people categorize all persons as being of one (and only one) of two (and only two) genders. They argued that this definition of gender (which also includes one's biological sex) is a social construction: that it is one way, *but not the only or even the most accurate way*, of perceiving reality. All of the normal questions posed about gender by scientists as well as the lay public (e.g., to what extent and how are the sexes different? what accounts for differences between them?), assume that gender constitutes a sharp dichotomy; that everyone fits one and only one category; and that one's gender is invariant. However, the reality is that "our seeing two genders" is what "leads to the 'discovery' of biological, psychological, and social differences," not vice versa (1978:163). They spent much of their book demonstrating that such assumptions do not, in fact, fit all the data available on the subject.

In describing the cultural assumption that there are two discrete genders only, Kessler and McKenna were describing a necessary underpinning of systems of gender stratification. Just about the first thing people do upon first meeting others is attribute a gender to them. Once gender is attributed, a person's subsequent behavior is interpreted in light of that definition and the definition becomes nearly impervious to change. While Kessler and McKenna did not go much beyond the attribution process in their analysis, it is easy to see that it stands as the logical starting point for inequitable treatment. To say that there is a system of gender inequality is to imply that, in their everyday encounters, females are treated inequitably by others, compared to males. Yet how can people be treated differently on the basis of their gender in the absence of an attribution of a gender to them? Thus, the cultural assumptions described by Kessler and McKenna, and a society's means of attributing gender, stand as the bedrock upon which a system of gender inequality is constantly reproduced in everyday life.

While we typically proclaim that gender attribution is a function of the genitals, in everyday life we rarely see the genitals of people before the attribution is done. Different societies emphasize different cues as relevant in making an attribution of gender. In turn, children begin learning their own society's cues at a relatively early age, and become more adept as they mature. Kessler and McKenna argued that in the Western world, we combine a number of cues into an assessment of gender, but within the general guideline of "see someone as female only when you cannot see them as male" (1978:158). However, this is not because maleness provides more obvious cues than femaleness. Rather: "The salience of male characteristics is a social construction. We construct gender so that male characteristics are *seen* as more obvious" (1978:159). Thus, male is the primary construction; the process of gender attribution creates and sustains an androcentric reality (1978:164).

Kessler and McKenna did not address the origins of the cultural assumptions they document or of our socially defined and transmitted techniques for attributing gender to individuals. The processes they described are taken as givens in the Western world. I therefore define them as phenomena that reflect, re-create, and sustain systems of gender inequality.

COMMUNICATION STUDIES

One very central aspect of Everyday Life theories is the study of normal speech, conversation, language usage, and nonverbal communication, topics examined as well by linguists and psychologists. This work tends to be empirical and descriptive, but underlying it is sometimes a more general theoretical orientation. In general, the focus has been upon how gender-specific ways of speaking, interacting conversationally, and communicating nonverbally, and how the structure of language itself, express and reinforce gender inequality. As linguist McConnell-Ginet put it, "social constraints on speech behavior may restrict women's and men's options and function in the social control of women. . . . Our speech not only reflects our place in culture and society but also helps to create that place" (1978:542).

Fishman

Pamela Fishman provided an example of this approach in a feminist analysis of verbal interaction between husbands and wives (1982). Her basic argument was that male-female power relations are expressed in conversation. She went on to opine that through conversation couples produce and sustain the reality of their relationship and of the world. Because the reality being produced reflects male power, the very inequality that generates this situation is reinforced.

Conversation requires that both parties be willing to participate; an attempt by one met by disinterest on the part of the other does not result in conversation (interaction). Fishman argued that women end up working at interaction because men often exercise their power by refusing to become full participants. Women employ a variety of strategies, such as asking a question or prefacing a statement with "this is interesting," in working at getting men to participate in an interaction. Women also support men in their conversation, encouraging it to continue. Given their superior power, men neither feel the need to begin conversations in ways other than by simple assertions, nor do they generally work at supporting women's conversation. Argued Fishman, women work harder than men because they are less certain of success. The result is that "the definition of what is appropriate conversation becomes the man's choice. What part of the world the interactants orient to, construct, and maintain the reality of, is his choice, not hers" (1982:178).

Interaction work appears natural for women because it is socially required of them. That women actually work in an unreciprocated fashion at supporting men conversationally is obscured by its apparent naturalness, and the maintenance of male-female power relations is hidden as well.

West and Zimmerman

West and Zimmerman (1977) devoted their attention to the phenomenon of conversational interruptions, that is, violations of normal turn-taking rules. They noted empirically that women and children are both more subject to interruption than adult males, implying that women have restricted rights to speak and may be ignored or interrupted at will. Specifically, according to West and Zimmerman, men interrupt women in order to display domination or control over them; in order to in fact control the behavior of women; and as a signal of "the presence of issues pertinent to the activation of dominating behavior by the male" (1977:528).

McConnell-Ginet

Sally McConnell-Ginet explored that aspect of speech called intonation, "the tunes to which we set the text of our talk," arguing that this may be "the chief linguistic expression in American English of femininity and masculinity, because it serves to underscore the gender identification of the participants in certain contexts of communication" (1978:542). She further suggested that intonation is especially important for understanding gender differences in speech strategies, that is, ways of using talk to achieve one's ends, and in the expression of attitudes and emotions. In turn, these are closely linked to power and social control. Feminine intonation is interpreted and evaluated from a masculine perspective; it is "apparently heard by the male-dominated ear of our culture as signaling women's relative instability (and from the male viewpoint, incompetence) and symbolizing her devalued 'naturalness'" (1978:542). In short, she argued that women's speech is discounted on the basis of how something is said rather than what the words mean. While intonational differences between the sexes arise from anatomical differences, nonetheless the nature and extent of the differences are significantly affected by cultural convention.

Lakoff

In her book *Language and Woman's Place* (1975), Robin Lakoff described a multitude of differences between American men's and women's languages. She argued that "the discrepancies that appear to exist are harmful to women's self-image and to the image people in general form of women's character and abilities" (1975:51). She singled out as central one underlying aspect of the variety of gender differences in language use: the ladylike or polite manner in which females, much more so than males, are taught to speak. Speaking in a polite, ladylike manner is rooted in a fear of appearing masculine and in person-oriented rather than object-oriented concerns. Major consequences of this speech style are a lack of assertiveness and an inability to be taken seriously.

Mayo and Henley

In addition to verbal interaction, gender-linked aspects of nonverbal communication have been analyzed in terms of their contribution to the maintenance of gender systems. Psychologists Mayo and Henley (1981) noted that nonverbal communication encodes power well, sending covert power messages through such mechanisms as gesture, movement, touch, gaze, and spatial arrangements. It therefore lends itself to the perpetuation of power differentials, including those rooted in gender (1981:8; see also Henley, 1977, for a detailed, mostly descriptive account of this phenomenon).

Gender-linked aspects of nonverbal behavior are resistant to personal and social change. Such behavior is usually unconscious and would have to be made conscious before it could be purposely altered. It is learned during early childhood socialization and therefore is likely to reflect traditional gender norms. Women, much more than men, are skilled at decoding nonverbal cues, especially those of males, because traditionally women are expected to adapt to the needs and styles of men. Mayo and Henley suggested that because this difference is a function of a power differential between males and females, nonverbal communication is unlikely to change until there is change in the distribution of power. They went on to suggest that women's traditional adaptability retards change in their own gender role, and that gender-deviant nonverbal behavior is punished. Gender inequality is constantly re-created by gender-specific forms of nonverbal behavior, which are very difficult to change without first reducing gender inequality.

FERGUSON

Working primarily from Mead's Symbolic Interactionist perspective, political scientist Kathy Ferguson also concentrated on the phenomenon of power as the major mechanism that perpetuates gender inequality, in her book *Self, Society, and Womankind* (1980). She defined power as "the ability of persons or groups to define the situation within which others must act" (1980:74). She then argued that all major social institutions tend to interlock and reinforce one another, so that those groups that have power in one, are likely to wield power in others. Morever, "the norms and rules of the generalized other that serve to reflect and legitimize such relations within one realm are likely to operate in a similar way in other realms as well" (1980:75).

Ferguson rejected the notion that any one kind of institution (family, economic, political, etc.) or type of variable can serve as a universal causal theory of sex inequality. She thus explicitly eschewed any attempt at a causal statement, focusing instead on accounting for how systems of domination, especially the domination of females by males, perpetuate themselves.

In a system of gender inequality, men possess the power not only to define specific situations, but also to define the generalized other — the basic standards, norms, and definitions of the collectivity. Since, according to Mead, a fundamental aspect of developing a self-concept is interacting with and internalizing the generalized other, "when women undergo this process . . . they are defining themselves by reference to standards that brand them as inferior" (1980:155). In adopting the generalized other, women are required to adopt a perspective toward themselves that discourages an autonomous self-definition. For women, the very process by which a self-identity is formed undermines that self-identity. The generalized other typically appears to societal members as natural and immutable. Women are thus unable to define the situations in which they act, or even define themselves in terms of their own experiences. Females are taught, by representatives of the very institutions which dominate them, that their troubles are private and individual, not social, and are to be solved within themselves rather than by political action:

> Power can be exercised most blatantly against those who have no defense because they have been convinced they deserve their subordination, because their problems are defined as within themselves. (1980:160)

Ferguson also argued that because of their powerlessness, women are forced to become highly adept at taking the role of the other—specifically, male others. They must be able to anticipate the requirements of men in order to avoid negative sanctions; they must manage emotional relationships in order to accomplish anything. In short, if one can act only through others, then a sensitivity to human context and interaction is essential (1980:161-2). Women (along with other powerless persons) also develop an orientation towards pleasing others—especially males—and they become dependent on approval from the more powerful male others. By pleasing, flattering, and acquiescing to men, women avoid punishment and are able to accomplish at least some of their aims. Part of this process is also learning to subordinate their own needs to the needs of others. This nurturant orientation is, of course, manifested in the domestic role. But domesticity within the context of the isolated nuclear family further reinforces women's inability to challenge the system, inasmuch as they lack any other adult perspective on their situation.

Ferguson was arguing that male power to define situations and the generalized other produces among females attributes of personality and behavior that are typical of the powerless in general. These attributes sustain both a flattering self-image for males and a low probability that women will have the psychic wherewithal to challenge the status quo.

GOFFMAN

Irving Goffman developed a general theoretical offshoot of Symbolic Interactionism known as the Dramaturgical approach (discussed briefly in chapter 1), which stressed the ways in which people construct and manage the impressions they make upon others in social interactions. He applied this approach to the topic of gender in an essay (1977) that focused on how contemporary Americans construct gender differentiation, and hence inequality. He began by stressing that the very slight biological differences between males and females are socially elaborated—with substantial work—into grounds for enormously different outcomes for members of each **sex class**. In order for this to happen, the society must develop a **social accounting**, that is, an integrated body of social beliefs and practices which is cohesive and all-embracing. Like Kessler and McKenna, Goffman located this in the beliefs that males and females are naturally, that is, biologically, radically different, and that all individuals can be placed in one and only one of the two categories.

Individuals are sorted into a sex class beginning at birth, and on the basis of that subjected to differential socialization. The result is that in all societies, there is a sex-class specific way of appearing, acting, and feeling, which is accompanied by a source of accounts that justify, explain, or disapprove the behavior of an individual. To the extent that "the individual builds up a sense of who and what he [sic] is by referring to his [sic] sex class and judging himself[sic] by the ideals of masculinity (or femininity), one may speak of gender identity" (1977:304).

Because males and females are socially defined as radically dissimilar, both require the specialized services of the other. For women, a stake is developed in the very organization—the family—which divides them from one another, because their resources flow primarily from males to whom they are attached as kin. Members of each sex are required to validate the gender identity of the other sex, each giving the other the opportunity to display those behaviors socially defined as specific to only one gender.

Goffman discussed in detail five phenomena that have the effect of confirming our gender stereotypes and the prevailing arrangement between the sexes: the sex-class division of labor; cross-sex siblings as socializers; toilet practices which segregate the sexes and provide different quality accommodations for each; the effects of appearance (youth and attractiveness) on job selection; and our identification system, namely, exaggerated differences in appearance, voice, naming, even handwriting that allow us to immediately assign gender to a stranger. He then reviewed several means by which irrelevant biological differences are converted into differences of vast social importance (1977:319). The first is the male use of physical force, which although infrequently employed among adults, stands as a metaphor or guiding imagery of masculinity and as antithetical to femininity. Likewise, sports are used as a basic expression of masculinity, as activities designed to allow males to manifest the qualities defined as basic to them. Yet another mechanism is the fact that while males and females are not, on the average, substantially different in strength and size, at the couple level males are nearly always superior to their partners in these and many other ways (e.g., education, occupational status, and income). This encourages a perception of much greater gender difference than exists. Goffman also examined playfulness as providing opportunities for the display of gender, and hence the reinforcement of perceptions of difference. Indeed, he argued that individuals actively seek out opportunities, which potentially exist in virtually all social environments, to display gender to others, thereby affirming their own gender identity. He singled out the management of talk as especially important in this regard, including who initiates conversation, turn-taking, who changes topics, to whose utterances attention is paid, and so on.

In all of these ways, Goffman was attempting to demonstrate that people are constantly involved in *producing* gender differentiation. In pursuing affirmation of a sense of identity, members of each sex do that which is defined as undoable (or not done well) by members of the other sex. For men, this entails demonstrations of strength and competence. However, for women it entails demonstrations of weakness, vulnerability, and ineptitude. The thrust of this theoretical argument is that it is in the minutiae of everyday social interaction that people constantly construct and reinforce social definitions of gender differentiation and inequality in their search to sustain their gendered self-identity.

HAAVIND

A similar theory was developed by Norwegian psychologist Hanne Haavind (1984), who examined how, in mutually confirming one another's gender through romantic love, men and women create male dominance within marriage. This, in turn, supports and legitimates the larger patriarchal system. Marriage does not cause gender inequality per se; rather, it is "embedded in a social system of uneven distributions" (1984:138).

Haavind saw masculinity and femininity not as sets of traits but as "an evaluation of how persons *relate* to one another" (1984:147). The basic normative expectation of the marital relationship is that of male dominance. Based on love, marriage in contemporary societies is an alliance for the mutual confirmation of gender between the partners. Within marriages, behaviors and decisions are in fact predicated on male dominance, but this is concealed by an ideology of mutual love. Both partners believe that their behavior and that of their partner is a result of free choice, including concern for the other rooted in love. In reality, however, such choices are patterned and systematically reflect male advantage. In this way, "marriage becomes a hidden disciplinary agency because of the major role of love in identity confirmation" (1984:149). After the romance wears off, loyalty replaces love in this function.

Haavind more explicitly defined the invisible, standard marital contract: the marital relationship is top priority for the wife but for the husband other relationships come first. If he does something for her, it is a favor, whereas for her the same behavior would be an obligation (cooking a meal). Conversely, if she places primary importance on another relationship (a friend, for instance), he is perceived as making a sacrifice. In short, given the implicit standard contract, each partner's behavior is interpreted through the prism of gender-specific expectations to the disadvantage of women. But this fact is hidden from both women and men, who typically see their own and their partner's behaviors as expression of free will and love. In this way, gender inequality is both legitimated and perpetuated.

WEST AND ZIMMERMAN

In a recent article, West and Zimmerman (1987) analyzed gender, not as a trait of individuals, but as something that is constantly being created in social interactions. Like Goffman, they argued that people organize their activities in order to express gender in a normative manner. Moreover, people are predisposed to interpret others' behaviors as expressions of gender. In turn, such behavior and interpretations create and, most importantly, legitimate gender itself. In this way gender-normative behavior comes to be perceived as natural and normal. For West and Zimmerman, virtually all activities can be, and typically are assessed according to their gender content. Behavior is constantly interpreted and evaluated according to the sex of the individual performer. They argued that therefore people cannot avoid "doing gender," although they may do it inappropriately, that is, nonnormatively. But in that case, they are suspect as individuals. Social control is exercised at the interactional level, with the result that males and females are typically constrained to behave in ways that are gender normative. They ended by asserting that the ongoing creation of gender in social interactions constitutes the scaffold upon which the social structural and cultural components of gender inequality are built.

SCHUR

Yet another offshoot of Symbolic Interactionism has been Labeling theory. Edwin Schur (1984) applied this to an analysis of women and argued that through the routine devaluation of women, general disparities in social and economic power between the sexes are reinforced. Yet in circular fashion, women's vulnerability to devaluation rests on their social subordination, that is, their poor power position. Labeling theorists argue that norms are established by those in power, and therefore definitions of deviance are as well. The powerful use stigmatization, that is, deviance-labeling, as a social control mechanism to keep the less powerful in their place. Schur's discussion therefore focused on the nature of the norms and deviances males define and apply to females, in an effort to maintain the gender status quo by which males benefit.

Schur began by defining gender as "a normative system, a pervasive network of interrelated norms and sanctions through which female (and male) behavior is evaluated and controlled" (1984:11). In everyday interactions people evaluate one another in terms of gender norms, and the reality or possibility of stigmatization for deviance constitutes a major control mechanism that backs up and enforces the restrictions and limitations placed on women.

According to Schur, as they apply to women, gender norms result in the overall devaluation of women for two basic reasons. First, the very fact of being female is a devalued status, carrying subtle kinds of stigma with it. Second, specific gender norms often place women in a no-win situation in which deviance is stigmatized and punished, but conformity brings few rewards. Indeed, conformity reinforces the very disadvantages entailed in their devalued status as women.

Stigma can accrue to what a person is as well as to what she or he does. Schur argued that femaleness is socially a master status, and a stigmatized one at that. **Master status** means that "women are perceived and reacted to at least initially, and often primarily, in terms of their femaleness. Only secondarily, if at all, do their other identities and qualities determine responses to them" (1984:25). In responding to a female on the basis of her master status, others tend to selectively perceive and depict that person in terms of stereotypes about that type of person. Contradictions to the stereotype go unnoticed or are defined as exceptions. Moreover, since behavior is interpreted by others on the basis of gender-based stereotypes, the same behavior by a man and a woman may be labeled very differently, being stigmatized for one but not the other. In particular, Schur argued that gender norm deviance, and even female victimization by males, are likely to be labeled by authorities as mental illness for women.

Because women are responded to on the basis of their membership in a devalued category, they are **objectified**. Schur claimed that they are not seen as unique individuals but rather as part of the category women. Objectification allows others to treat the stigmatized individuals in exploitative and degrading ways. In response, women often feel like they are being treated like a thing rather than a person. Objectification is closely related to gender norms which pertain to women's appearance, sexuality, and the types of specific social roles deemed appropriate for them. Schur discussed a large number of ways in which women are stigmatized by breaking informal norms pertaining to such things as weight, sexual conduct, the decision whether to marry or have children, and so on. In addition to the overall stigma of their femaleness, perhaps most women feel devalued by their failure to completely live up to the array of specific gender norms. Female objectification also comprises the root cause of male sexual harassment, rape, and battering of women; of their use of female prostitutes; and of their consumption of pornography. The fact that males are infrequently stigmatized or punished for these behaviors also reflects the objectified, devalued status of women, as well as the fact that it is males who make and enforce laws pertinent to such behavior. Indeed, female victims of harassment, rape, and abuse are often defined as responsible for the male behavior in question, and are thus doubly victimized and further stigmatized.

The result of this pervasive devaluation and objectification of women is often the creation of a self-fulfilling prophecy by which women come to see themselves as inferior. Low self-esteem, withdrawal, passivity, in-group (other women) hostility, and identification with the oppressors (men) are other responses to devaluation. Seeking whatever rewards are available, women accommodate the system by immersing themselves in their own, segregated world, and by displaying stereotyped femininity in interactions with males. In all these ways, women come to inadvertently contribute to the maintenance of the system that devalues them.

KASPER

The general theories which together comprise the Everyday Life approach were called **Interpretive theory** by Anne Kasper (1986). She argued that these theories have failed to perceive an inherent conflict that women experience between the culturally given and experientially derived types of self-reflection. She suggested that a major result of such conflict within the context of a male-defined social life is that women fail to acquire the capacities to meet contemporary standards of achievement and competence.

Calling upon theory and research from several different sociological and psychological approaches, Kasper argued that "females . . . know self through others. Males . . . know self more through objective achievements . . . " (1986:38). However, women's superior ability to relate genuinely with others, their emotional labor, is taken for granted, undervalued, and often misused. Women's sense of self is integrally bound to these affiliative qualities. In turn

> this derivative status and identity . . . leaves women defined by others, unsure of who they are, dependent upon others for their sense of well-being and competence, and denied an integrated autonomous identity of their own. (1986:40)

Women's lives come to be taken up with the existence of others.

> Bound to the dailiness of human activity and the fleeting behaviors and emotions of the moment, women may fail to develop those capacities required for the abstractions of larger projects and the sustained efforts of long-term goals and endeavors. (1986:40)

In short, women's way of understanding the self encourages and creates capacities that restrict their horizons and competence in the public sphere.

These attributes reflect the culturally given meaning of self offered to women, and Kasper argued that they represent only a portion of women's consciousness. Every person has a unique biography as well, hence a portion of their identity is likewise unique. Each person thus comes to an understanding of self as both an object created by imposed cultural meanings and as a subject and autonomous being. Kasper posited that for women, the subjective self, rooted in individual experience, is autonomous, able to make choices, to take action. This self is in conflict with the culturally derived self. In turn, as suggested above, such conflict may further contribute to women's incapacity to develop traits deemed important to achievement in the public domain.

SUMMARY

Despite the substantial diversity in emphasis in the Everyday Life theories, one theme pervades most of them: superior male power shapes interactions between the sexes in ways that reinforce male superiority, especially by allowing males to define the reality of the situation and control the content of the interaction. Conversely, gender norms for females shape their behaviors and responses in interactions with males in ways that reinforce their inferior status to the extent that they conform; moreover, as Schur pointed out, those same norms result in stigmatization for women when they fail to conform. A secondary theme present in many of these theories concerns the active efforts people make to sustain a gendered self-image when interacting with members of the other sex. Everyday Life theories argue, in effect, that people are constantly working at constructing a sense of a gendered self, as well as working at attributing gender to others. In accomplishing this work, people perpetuate the existing gender system.

SUMMARY AND CONCLUSIONS

The theories reviewed in this chapter all presuppose the existence of gender stratification, at least implicitly, and focus on the mechanisms that contribute to its maintenance and intergenerational reproduction. Two types of feminist theories, the neo-Freudian and Socialization, address the question of how new generations become gendered members of their society, that is, take on the gender attributes of the previous generation. These approaches at least tacitly assume that by adulthood people differ by gender on traits relevant to acquiring and playing adult roles. They therefore state or imply that systems of gender inequality are maintained by the early childhood processes by which people become gendered. Some of the eclectic approaches (especially Kanter) reject this view, arguing that gender differences are produced *among adults* by the system which allocates different and unequal roles to men and women. In turn, the attitudes and behaviors generated by differential power, opportunity, and so on affect future opportunities, producing a self-perpetuating cycle.

The Everyday Life theories share with the structural theories an emphasis on superior male power as a key variable in sustaining systems of gender stratification. For the Marxist-feminist and several eclectic structural theories, power is conceptualized primarily in terms of superior resources (especially economic) that enable men to have their way. These approaches also tend to emphasize the importance of ideology in legitimating such power and thereby producing among members of both sexes widespread agreement on the rightness of male superiority. The Everyday Life theories are more concerned with male power to define situations, establish standards of judgement, and thereby construct people's sense of social reality in ways conducive to maintaining a definition of the superiority of maleness among members of both sexes.

Macro- and microtheories from a variety of perspectives emphasize the importance of gender norms in perpetuating systems of gender inequality. Gender norms refer to social expectations that males and females will each behave in specific ways and enact or give priority to some specific social roles but not others. Such norms are presumably enforced by stigmatizing and punishing deviance. Many theories reviewed in this chapter emphasized that female gender norms tend to encourage domesticity, personal traits and behaviors antithetical to extradomestic achievement, and deference to males. In the words of both Fox and Lakoff, female gender norms encourage women to be ladies. In so doing, such norms pressure females into behaviors that reinforce their subordinate position. In addition, gender norms permit and encourage differential treatment of the sexes, thereby reproducing unequal opportunity to perform various social roles.

Finally, the most recurrent theme in this chapter, to be found in virtually every type of theory, is that the very fact of gender inequality produces mechanisms that function to reproduce such inequality. While they differ substantially in which processes they emphasize, all the theories see maintenance mechanisms as fundamentally embedded in the workings of the gender system itself. Gender stratification therefore continuously reproduces itself in a manner that appears automatic. The question for the next chapter is: what else do systems of gender inequality produce?

4 SOCIAL CONSEQUENCES OF GENDER STRATIFICATION

In the last chapter, theoretical approaches were reviewed that address the question: How are systems of gender inequality maintained? Another way of phrasing this same question is: What are the *consequences* of gender differentiation and inequality? In this chapter attention is focused on the consequences of gender systems on aspects of social life other than gender, which include such things as economic and political structures and practices, societal values and priorities, cultural beliefs, and the general well-being of children and families. As we shall see, however, few of these issues have been explored to any significant extent.

MARXIST-FEMINIST EXPLANATIONS

In previous chapters, discussions of Marxist-feminist theories have repeatedly emphasized the mutual relatedness and supportiveness of capitalism and patriarchy. Clearly, for these theorists a major consequence of gender stratification is the bolstering of capitalist systems and therefore of social class stratification. This occurs because of several specific aspects of patriarchy.

Eisenstein's analysis of women's oppression (1979) explicitly delineated that which many of the other Marxist-feminists implied, often less explicitly: that female oppression functions as a major support of capitalist systems. She argued that in being responsible for domestic work, women reproduce new workers necessary for the labor force; work in the labor force for lower wages, thereby presumably enhancing capitalists' profits (see also Sacks, 1974); and stabilize the economy through their role as consumers (Eisenstein, 1979:29). Vogel (1983) implied the first two consequences also, as well as another: maintenance of the existing (male) labor force, which in turn frees more of its time to produce surplus value, that is, profits, for capitalists. Hartmann (1979:228-9) argued that a sex-segregated labor force exacerbates sex divisions and thereby weakens working class unity that could threaten to overturn the capitalist system. Indeed, capitalists may use patriarchal benefits to buy the allegiance of male workers to capitalism.

SOKOLOFF

Natalie Sokoloff (1980) provided perhaps the most complete discussion of this issue. Like several others, she argued that gender inequality in the labor force serves capitalists' interests because it keeps the sexes divided and competing with one another, rather than combining in a unified struggle against capitalism. In addition, capitalism is able to use women to cheapen the cost of male labor. In examining the kinds of work women do, Sokoloff found further ways in which the capitalist system profits from the gender system. Many social needs are not amenable to profit making. "Women's . . . nurturance, supportiveness, and emotional sensitivity serve social needs well. Thus, women's labor . . . supports social connection outside of private profit-making enterprises, in the home and through government services" (1980:211). More specifically in terms of paid labor,

> much of women's work in health, in social services, in education, and in other government bureaucracies is paid for out of the taxes of . . . employees—the costs are socialized at the expense of the working class—but the work serves to the benefit of capital. (1980:211-2)

Sokoloff also suggested that the gender system contributes to the reproduction of the social class system, because women play an essential role in articulating the family to the larger society. In part, they do this through their role as primary consumer, in part as primary child-socializer and family social secretary:

> women tend to maintain family living spaces with the appropriate stratification symbols and life-styles; to arrange friendships for their children, husbands, and themselves . . . ; and to articulate the fam-

ily and its members to the class-, gender-, and racially appropriate bureaucratic, educational, professional, and retailing organizations. . . . All this is in addition to the . . . notion that women reproduce class . . . through socializing children and husbands with the appropriate culture, ideologies, attitudes, and habits. (1980:225)

Sokoloff reached the conclusion that "without women's work . . . as constructed by patriarchy and capitalism today, neither male wage labor, surplus value for the capitalist, nor social classes would be possible" (1980:223).

WARD

Ward's (1984) feminist revision of World-Systems theory explained how economic dependency reduces the status of women, relative to men, in peripheral nations (see chapter 2 in this book). The subtitle of that work also included the impact of the world system on fertility. Peripheral nations tend to be societies of high fertility levels and rapidly increasing population. These facts help to maintain—indeed often to increase—their level of poverty. Ward argued that by decreasing women's economic opportunities relative to men's, foreign investment and trade dependency also increase women's motivation in peripheral societies to have large families, thereby sustaining high fertility rates. Women confined to subsistence agriculture and petty trade find that children constitute an economic asset, because they can help out at a very early age, and contribute economically later in life as well. Moreover, confined to traditional social roles and excluded from education, women maintain traditional values concerning motherhood and lack the knowledge to take advantage of modern contraception. To the extent that women's status suffers from national economic dependency, then, the nation's fertility rate will remain high, in turn decreasing the possibility of that nation escaping poverty and economic dependency. In addition, argued Ward, because women contribute less to the national economy than they could, their depressed status leads directly to lowered rates of economic growth and heightened income inequality.

ECLECTIC STRUCTURAL THEORIES

Among the Marxist-feminists, Sokoloff made an especially clear statement linking patriarchy to the intergenerational reproduction of social class. In a brief, but seminal essay, role theorist Rose Laub Coser (1975) made the same basic point. She did so by focusing on a largely ignored phenomenon in sociology: the relationship between spatial and social mobility.

COSER

Coser began by arguing that "the use of physical space is typically linked to the regulation of social relations" (1975:471). Traditionally, the most important function of the family has been to locate its members in the social stratification hierarchy. A man contributes his occupational status to this, while a woman contributes through her control over the scheduled activities of family members, both at home and elsewhere. As long as family members', and especially children's, whereabouts are predictable and controlled, family status can be maintained. "It is through the mother, who gives primacy to the place of residence, that the kinship system is integrated with the stratification system" (1975:472). In brief, mothers control the social contacts of their children by controlling their spatial movement, thereby protecting familial social status.

Movement in space that is not controlled insulates individuals from observability and control and has the potential of expanding peoples' role-sets. The new role partners may not be desirable from the point of view of the family, thus resulting in potential disturbance of familial status. Conversely, spatial movement may enhance status by expanding role-sets to encompass higher status individuals.

Coser argued that women are largely denied opportunities to travel, hence to expand their own role-sets. Occupations involving travel are largely confined to men, while women maintain the family as a permanent institution by remaining at home and available to its members. Not only is the individual woman's upward mobility thereby restricted, thus reinforcing the gender stratification system, but spatial restrictions on women as a group reinforce the existing social stratification system as well.

HOLTER

In several places in her analysis of gender differentiation in contemporary Western societies, Holter (1970) suggested systemic consequences. Gender differentiation refers to the allocation of different tasks to males and females. Such gender-specific specialization may contribute to greater overall efficiency, ensuring that various tasks are accomplished. However, it may also function in exactly the opposite manner:

> To the extent that it diminishes substitutability among role incumbents with different . . . specialized training, increases status incongruities, diminishes the number of conditions under which the capacities of some people can be used, and undermines the basis for communication and identification within the system. (1970:21)

Holter argued that there is an optimal amount of specialization: too much and role incumbents cannot be shifted in times of crisis; too little and efficiency is undermined. Although specialization need not be rooted in gender, when it is, it can improve efficiency if the degree of gender differentiation is not excessive.

As one type of ascriptive differentiation, gender may contribute to general social stability, although it may also, under certain circumstances, contain the seeds of change (a topic for the next chapter). Holter argued that social stability is rooted in predictability. Because gender is a stable individual trait, gender differentiation permits extensive predictability of peoples' behavior. Learned very early in life, gender differentiated modes of thinking and behaving are especially resistant to change, thereby reinforcing predictability and social stability. Allocation of tasks according to ascription is virtually automatic, requiring little decision making or individual assessment. In this way, time and energy are saved. Conflict and competition resulting from conflicting claims are minimized, all of which enhances social stability — at least in the short run.

Gender differentiation gives rise to gender stratification, by which men possess extensive power to influence the decisions made in most sectors of society. One result of this is that the "premises underlying the more uniquely masculine activities of business and political decision-making . . . will be different from the premises that underlie decision-making in the family." Holter suggested that intergenerational problems and conflicts may in part be a consequence of this difference (1970:220). She further suggested that it is because nondomestic social institutions reflect masculine values, that an overwhelming and lopsided orientation to instrumentality, rationality, transformation, efficiency, even violence characterizes contemporary social life. Moreover, because women are assumed to care for the home and family members while men are the chief breadwinners, it is possible for economic and political organizations to define familial responsibilities as irrelevant. This contributes to the sharp separation of the family from other social spheres. As a result of this and the fact that masculine values shape public decision making, children's interests tend to be unrepresented in industrialized societies. When public decisions of importance to children are made, they are made by those with the least contact with children — men.

One final social consequence of gender differentiation discussed by Holter, like that of other theorists already discussed, concerns social stratification. She argued that since children learn at an early age that one form of ascriptive differentiation and stratification is legitimate and proper (gender), they are prepared to accept the propriety of other forms, such as ascribed social class. She suggested that gender differentiation therefore affects "not social stratification as such, but the principles [ascribed or achieved] on which stratification is based" (1970:228).

In an intriguing essay on conflict between and within genders, Karen Rosenblum (1986) claimed that the key feature of American gender definitions is a dichotomy between caring (feminine) and autonomy (masculine). Her discussion of the masculine role is relevant here. An ethic of autonomy, she argued, entails protection from interference from others and the right to self-fulfillment. Logically, this presumes equality and would appear to militate against the creation of hierarchy and the exercise of dominance. Yet the outcome is precisely the opposite. Why? By valuing differentiation and separation, the right to do as one pleases, masculinity requires opposition to the social world. This, then, becomes the background from which men differentiate themselves. The need to differentiate the self promotes stratification and asocial, even antisocial behavior (1986:100). Although the terminology varies, we have seen that many theorists suggest that the same type of gender dichotomy is widespread cross-culturally—Rosenblum's argument may have substantially broader applicability than she suggests. It is interesting to note that she has used a different theoretical approach to reach essentially the same conclusions as the Marxist-feminists and Holter.

MEEKER AND WEITZEL-O'NEILL

One final structural approach is Meeker and Weitzel-O'Neill's (1985) theory of male advantage in small groups, which was reviewed briefly in chapter 3. Recall that they argued that men, but not women, are legitimated in an attempt to raise their status within a group. One outcome of this is that often

> groups of women had difficulty with a task because no one wanted to take the lead in coordinating activities, groups of men had difficulty . . . because everyone tried to take the lead. . . . It appears that when either men or women in a task-oriented group operate according to stereotyped sex role expectations, they are more likely to hinder than to help coordination. (1985:399)

ANTHROPOLOGICAL THEORIES

Anthropological theories often stress cultural values as central variables. The two brief discussions I located relevant to this chapter manifest this orientation. Sanday's (1981) account of the origins of male dominance included a brief suggestion of one general social consequence of the gender system. Recall from chapter 2 that her theory stressed the central importance of cultural configuration in determining the extent of male dominance. In addition to that outcome, her theory proposed that an inner, feminine configuration, rooted in a creation myth involving females, results in a prevalence of cooperation over competition in human affairs. The converse presumably applies to an outer, male cultural configuration with a male-dominated creation myth. The overall emphasis on cooperation versus competition in a society is rooted in the same gender-related idea system that produces that society's system of sex stratification.

Collier and Rosaldo (1981) developed a theory to account for conceptions of gender and the relative gender equality in hunting and gathering societies. They argued that the only basis of inequality among men in such societies is marital status. They posited that the fact (recognized by many anthropologists) that people in these societies show no interest in accumulating material possessions, indeed, often appear as quite lazy, can also be understood from their theoretical perspective. In hunting and gathering societies, there is no leader with the power to directly stop conflicts among members. If one owns something, that person must protect it from others. For a man, failure to protect a material possession will suggest to others that he cannot protect his most important possession: his claim to his wife (the source of his status as an adult). Therefore, a man will give away valuables rather than face a lonely life of perpetual fighting or the risk that other men will define him as unable to keep them from appropriating his possessions (1981:298). Since they pass on material objects as gifts to others, they are unwilling to invest much time or effort in accumulating them.

MICROINTERACTIONAL APPROACHES

Given the paucity of theoretical statements relevant to the societal consequences of gender stratification, the few microlevel theories available are collected in one section of this chapter.

NEO-FREUDIAN FEMINISTS: CHODOROW AND KITTAY

Chodorow's feminist revision of Psychoanalytic theory shares with the Marxist-feminists an emphasis on the perpetuation of capitalism as a major consequence of the gender system. This occurs because of the psychological conditioning of males to participate in, and thereby reinforce, the capitalist world of work (1978:181 and 186; see also Chodorow, 1979). She argued that regardless of social class or particular occupation, contemporary capitalist production requires "conformity to behavioral rules and external authority, predictability and dependability, the ability to take on others' values and goals as one's own." Together, these "reflect an orientation external to oneself and one's own standards, a lack of autonomous and creative self-direction." This type of personality, in turn, is produced best in nuclear, isolated, neolocal families in which women are the overwhelming child-rearers (1978:186).

Because contemporary mothers are so heavily invested in their maternal role and children are almost totally nurtured by that one person, gratification flows to young children almost exclusively from their mothers. Boys must relinquish their dependence on their mothers, but in so doing, Chodorow argued, "they retain an unconscious sense that there is one finally satisfying prize to be won." As a result, males turn their lives into a search for success that will prove their independence and win their mothers' approval (1978:188). But they have no inner sense of goals or real autonomy and therefore they tend to accept and conform to the dictates and requirements that confront them at work. This same family structure also produces a manipulative personality which lends itself to modern capitalism; to media and product consumerism; and to the legitimation of a polity that serves people unequally. She concluded:

> Exclusive maternal involvement and the extension of dependence create a generalized need to please and to "succeed," and a seeming independence. This need to succeed can help to make someone dependable and reliable. Because it is divorced from specific goals and real inner standards but has involved the maintenance of an internal dependent relationship, it can also facilitate the taking of others' goals as one's own, producing the pseudo-independent organization man. (1978:189–90)

Chodorow contrasted this contemporary process, and the male personality that results from it, with that characteristic of an earlier period of capitalist development when individual goals were important for more men, and entrepreneurial achievement as well as worker discipline were based more on inner moral direction and repression. In that era, boys had greater contact with their fathers, the mother-child bond was therefore less exclusive, and fathers were more authoritative. She argued that the result was that sons could internalize their father's authority through a classic oedipal struggle. They thus developed greater inner direction and self-motivation (1978: 188–9).

In another theory derived from the Freudian approach, Kittay's theory of womb envy (1983) included as one type of defense mechanism the stifling of feelings of love and intensification of hate (see chapter 2). While most of her discussion was in terms of men's feelings towards women, there is the implication that this involves a more general glorification of destruction (1983:117). It is only a small step to draw the conclusion that Kittay would lay at the feet of male womb envy, hence of systems of female subordination, the blame for war, environmental destruction, and most other forms of human violence.

In Chapter 3, Goffman's (1977) Dramaturgical account of the social production of gender was reviewed. One of the mechanisms he discussed was the
socialization of siblings. He argued that male and female children learn in the
family setting that differential treatment and rewards accrue on the basis of
sex-class, that regardless of the social ranking of the family compared to
other families, females are subordinate to males. The result is that "the
deepest sense of what one is — one's gender identity — is . . . given its initial
character from ingredients that do not bear on ethnicity or socio-economic
stratification. . . . " As a result, "we all acquire a deep capacity to shield
ourselves from what we gain and lose by virtue of our placement in the overall social hierarchy." Moreover, regardless of how subordinated a man might
be at work, all men come home to a sphere in which they dominate. Said
Goffman, "Gender, not religion, is the opiate of the masses" (1977:315). Like
the Marxist-feminists, but less explicitly and in less detail, Goffman implied
that class consciousness and collective action are impeded by the gender system, that the economic status quo is bolstered by the fact that male advantage
over females distracts them from their own socioeconomic plight.

EXCHANGE THEORY: CHAFETZ

I developed an Exchange theory model (1980b) to explain marital dissolution
rates, which argued that the greater the degree of equality between spouses,
the more likely their marriages would dissolve. I began by claiming that
when conflicts over scarce and valued resources (e.g., money, time, energy)
arise between spouses, four potential strategies are available to each in their
attempts to gain compliance from the other: authority, control, influence,
and manipulation. Authority requires that the incumbent of one role be considered by both partners as the legitimate decision maker. It is bolstered by
law, custom, and religion. Control requires that one partner have superior
resources that can be used to threaten or bribe the other into compliance.
Money is probably the most important resource for control. Influence is
based on superior knowledge that can be used to persuade the other to comply. Manipulation entails the use of behaviors calculated to elicit a certain response from the other person, without the other being conscious of the
process.

I then posited that there is a rank order to these four strategies in terms of
the costs and rewards attaching to their use. Authority is the least costly and
most rewarding, followed by control, then influence, with manipulation being the most costly and least potentially rewarding strategy. I assumed that
people generally want to win conflicts, especially those that are zero-sum and
therefore not amenable to compromise, and that they will use the most

potentially rewarding and least costly strategy to do so that is within their ability.

Where superior authority or control exists, it almost always resides in husbands, because both are supported by extradomestic social institutions. In these cases, wives must rely on influence or manipulation and will generally lose. They will, however, tend to lack the economic wherewithal to leave the marriage — that must be provided by the broader society. Where males and females are equal in authority and control, both spouses will be forced to use influence and possibly manipulation. For husbands, equality is thus more costly and less rewarding, providing a strong impetus to leave marriages in response to conflict. However, wives do not come to use different strategies in situations of equality than in those of inequality. Thus there is no change in their reward/cost calculus, although they are likely to have the economic wherewithal to leave. The net result is an increase in the rate of marital dissolution as the relative status of the sexes becomes more equal in a society. In terms of the issue raised in this chapter, the logic of my theory suggests that one consequence of gender inequality is high rates of marital stability (although not intimate or fulfilling spousal relationships; see Chafetz, 1985).

SUMMARY AND CONCLUSIONS

The social consequence of gender stratification discussed most frequently by feminist theorists concerns the ways in which gender inequality and differentiation bolster the capitalist system and class stratification. This argument has been made not only by Marxist-feminists, but in several eclectic structural theories (Coser, Holter, Rosenblum), by a neo-Freudian (Chodorow), and by an Everyday Life sociologist (Goffman). A secondary theme argued that male dominance results in societal values that glorify competition rather than cooperation (Sanday), and antisocial, destructive, and even violent behavior (Rosenblum, Holter, Kittay). This has been a central theme of feminist movement ideology. It appears less central for the concerns of feminist social scientific theorists. There was some suggestion that social efficiency, predictability, and stability are enhanced by gender inequality — at least in the short run (Holter, Chafetz), although Holter also suggested that the opposite results may occur (also Meeker and Weitzel-O'Neill). Finally, Holter explicitly argued that gender stratification negatively affects public policy in terms of the needs of children and families. Arguments by Marxist-feminists discussed in earlier chapters manifest a similar concern with a short-shrifting of social needs under patriarchal capitalism.

It is apparent from the brevity of this chapter that most feminist theorists have not devoted attention to examining the ramifications of gender differentiation and stratification for other aspects of social life. Those who have, have done so briefly and in passing. Gender stratification is treated theoretically as a dependent variable to be explained, but rarely as an independent one that can explain other features of the social landscape. Feminist social scientists typically agree that the gender system constitutes a centrally important phenomenon in social life. Yet, to date, no one has attempted to thoroughly and systematically delineate how it shapes other aspects of collective existence. This points to a major gap in our knowledge that should be rectified. In fact, it is possible that many of the social consequences of gender inequality are sufficiently negative or dysfunctional for collective well-being that political capital could be gained for the feminist cause by adequately demonstrating them.

5 CHANGING SYSTEMS OF GENDER INEQUALITY

Central to my definition of feminist theory in chapter 1 was the criterion that it could be used to challenge or change a status quo that disadvantages women. To be a feminist is to be change oriented. Some of the theories reviewed in the preceding three chapters included innate, biological sex differences as a variable in their analyses, yet in no case was gender inequality itself thought to be immutable. All concurred in the view that human beings collectively create systems of gender stratification. If they create them, then they ostensibly have the collective ability to change them. Nonetheless, not all feminist theories explicitly include considerations of change toward greater equality. Moreover, the ability of the various theories to generate logically consistent strategies for such change is variable. Just as various theories present a plethora of sources of gender inequality or mechanisms supporting such inequality, it will become apparent that there are also many approaches concerning change.

In this chapter, two issues concerning social change toward greater gender equality will be considered. Each theory implies, if indeed it doesn't explicitly state, *what* fundamental aspect(s) of social life is (are) most important to change first in order to produce gender equality. In each case, some one or more mechanisms are identified as central to producing or reproducing inequality and therefore of prime importance in changing the status quo. Second is the issue of *how* such change can be brought about. What kinds of strategies are implied or offered by each theoretical approach in order to at least begin the change process in whatever variable(s) that theory designates as top priority? Many theories fail to address this issue or address it in a manner that is not logically consistent with the rest of the theory.

MARXIST-FEMINIST EXPLANATIONS

Most Marxist-feminist theorists maintain the classical Marxian emphasis on the need to create a classless society in order to realize gender equality. However, they simultaneously recognize that gender inequality persists in existing socialist systems. Classlessness is thus seen as a necessary but not sufficient step toward gender equality. Most of the theories reviewed in earlier chapters fail to offer explicit, theoretically derived statements about what, exactly, must happen after the demise of capitalism in order to achieve the end of female oppression. However, since all focus on women's privatized, domestic role as the root of their patriarchal oppression, it is safe to assume that this would constitute a major target of change.

SACKS

Marxist anthropologist Karen Sacks (1974) was more explicit in her discussion of what would have to occur to eliminate patriarchy. Recall from chapter 2 that for Sacks, the root of female oppression is to be found in the fact that women lack social adulthood. In turn, this results from their exclusion from social production for exchange, and confinement to domestic, or use-value production. Even where women enter the labor force, they remain responsible for domestic production, the maintenance of self and other exchange workers, and the rearing of future exchange workers. In this situation wage labor is little more than an additional burden added to their domestic responsibilities. The solution, according to Sacks, is for both sexes to do the same work, specifically, the production of social use-values. For this to occur,

> family and society cannot remain separate *economic* spheres of life. Production, consumption, child rearing, and economic decision making all need to take place in a single social sphere. . . . That is, what is now private family work must become public work for women to become full social adults. (1974:222)

Unlike many other feminist theorists who argue that women must enter the public realm, and men the domestic sphere for equality to result, Sacks was arguing that the domestic sphere and production for use-value must be converted into social labor and production for exchange.

Vogel

Vogel (1983) also located the roots of women's oppression within capitalist systems in women's domestic labor, and additionally in their lack of equal rights. She further argued that women's involvement in domestic labor, while reduced in recent years, cannot be abolished under capitalism because it would be too costly to do so. A socialist system is clearly required by Vogel's analysis, but it must be a socialist system that is fully attentive to the issues she has delineated. Complete equality of rights between the sexes must exist, but this is not sufficient. Domestic labor must be maximally socialized, and the remaining residue must be equally shared by men and women and even children. Stated otherwise, men and women alike have to be equally involved in social production regardless of the specific division of labor. Vogel recognized that existing socialist societies have generally failed to seriously confront this issue of domestic labor, hence they have failed to deal adequately with women's subordination. She went one step further. For women to become equal, she argued, women's rights would have to be unequal in some ways. They would require maternity leaves, lighter work in advanced pregnancy, and rest periods during times of menstruation in order to provide "the material conditions for women's full participation in all areas of social life" (1983:174). Vogel's argument is that the biological facts which have historically served to make women responsible for domestic labor in class societies must be compensated for if women are to be fully equal participants in social life. To do so requires a classless society in which no group can gain profit from women's subordination.

Ward

Recall from chapter 2 that Ward (1984) posited a series of intervening variables that link the independent variables, levels of foreign investment and trade dependency, to the relative status of women. In recent decades, increasing rates of those independent variables have generally worked to reduce the status of women in peripheral nations due to the expansion of world capitalism. In her conclusion Ward argued that reversing this trend and increasing the degree of gender equality within peripheral nations can be brought about by governmental action.

Policymakers should examine the effects of traditional investment policies and programs on women's access to the labor force to ensure that they are not placed at a competitive disadvantage with men. Transnational corporation (TNC) investment should be structured to provide a maximum of long-term and productive employment for women. Long-term employment alternatives must be provided for women in the event that corporations remove their factories to another country, as they often do. Nations need to guarantee humane treatment and opportunities to workers involved in TNC employment, while working with other nation-states in the region to prevent runaway plants. TNC employment should also be stabilized through equal employment practices, notices of layoff, and compensation for unemployed TNC workers. Ward also suggested that governments in peripheral nations should encourage the growth of labor-intensive production for import substitution in order to reduce trade dependency. In addition, women should be allowed access to union organization and protective legislation and should be involved in all facets of production, including management, so that they will be able to acquire skills that can be transferred to other employment settings (1984:149).

In short, Ward suggested that reversing the relationship between economic dependency and the declining status of women relative to men is possible if governments in peripheral nations would take steps to control the intervening mechanisms that create that relationship. Unanswered is the question of why such governments, which according to Ward's theory are male dominated and rooted in patriarchal relations, would be motivated to do so. While the long-run impact of such policies may be a general improvement in the economic fortunes of the entire nation, men's *relative* advantage over women would presumably decrease in both the short and long run. Given this probable result, it is unlikely that governments will take it upon themselves to establish the kinds of policies Ward suggests. In peripheral nations, female disadvantage provides male advantage both locally and to core-nation capitalists — a powerful combination!

HARTMANN

Heidi Hartmann (1984) explicitly recognized that males are unlikely to willingly relinquish their advantages. She concluded her analysis with a strong assertion that males, no matter how committed to the struggle against capitalism, cannot be expected or relied upon to relinquish their patriarchal privileges. As she stated about a feminist-socialist revolution, "Men have more to lose then their chains" (1984:188). Moreover, given their dual oppression under patriarchy and capitalism, women "have learned to understand what human interdependence and needs are. While men have long struggled *against* capital, women know what to struggle *for*" (1984:188, emphasis in the original). Therefore, women must develop their own organizations and power bases in the dual struggle against patriarchy and capitalism in search of a more humane society dedicated to serving social needs.

SUMMARY

Despite the fact that classical Marxist theory is preeminently a theory of social change, the Marxist-feminist theorists have failed to devote serious attention to the issue of change. *What* has to change from their perspective is clear: the relegation of women to domestic use-value production. To be equals, women and men must be equally involved in social labor and equally involved in whatever private labor remains. *How* this is to come about is not addressed, except to note that women must do it on their own. Given the Marxist-feminist emphasis on women's relative isolation within nuclear families, their double duty as exploited wage laborer and domestic worker, their relative lack of resources, and their ideological conservatism, it is difficult to see how they could organize with sufficient strength to overthrow patriarchy. Classical Marxism speaks of the revolutionary overthrow of capitalism by the proletariat. But the proletariat is a numerically enormous class, the bourgeoisie relatively small. Clearly, women confront men as nearly equal-sized groups. Nor have women's groups historically manifested any tendency towards violence. Finally, many Marxist-feminists end their essays or books with a brief discussion of the need for continued consciousness-raising to make women aware of their oppression. This, however, does not substitute for a theory of change, because the issue of how such consciousness will lead to social structural change goes undiscussed.

ANTHROPOLOGICAL APPROACHES

SCHELEGEL

Schlegel's (1977) multidimensional, anthropological approach to explaining variation in gender stratification systems was reviewed in chapter 2. She argued that the root of female disadvantage is to be found in male domination of central institutions in a society. In simple societies, typically the procreative and productive functions are both based in the domestic unit and share equal importance. With societal complexity, and especially industrialization, come the separation of these and the elevation of the productive to the status of central institution. Schlegel argued that if one takes the long view, this separation can be a positive factor in producing gender equality. This is because there is no longer any requirement for the division of labor by sex. Since economic institutions ignore procreation, they have no logic upon which to base such a division. In industrial societies, women's status, like men's, depends on their role in the public sector rather than the domestic. However, this serves to create a conflict for women, because primary responsibility for children still rests with them. This responsibility inevitably restricts their ability to attain highly rewarded positions in the public sphere.

Changing Systems of Gender Inequality 131

In short, the nuclear family militates against female success by granting to women with children less time, energy, and freedom of movement than to men. The logical change strategy that flows from this is to create social arrangements that allow for both the care of children and greater freedom for mothers from childrearing responsibilities. In concrete terms, Schlegel referred to greater father involvement, nurseries, communal households with dispersed childcare responsibilities, and the flexibility to experiment (1977:36–7).

ROSALDO

Rosaldo (1974) presented a very similar theory. Recall from chapter 2 her argument that women's subordination is rooted in the division of labor by which women function in the domestic, men in the public spheres of social life. She suggested that women are least subordinated where the two spheres are relatively undifferentiated, or in highly differentiated societies where women enter the public sphere and men the domestic. In modern societies, like the United States, the domestic and public spheres are sharply differentiated. She argued in her conclusion that if more than a few elite women are to enter the public world, the nature of work itself will have to be altered and the asymmetry between work and the home reduced. This, in turn, requires that men take on new responsibility at home and in childcare (1974:42).

FRIEDL

Friedl (1975) also located the causes of gender inequality in the gender division of labor, but she emphasized the fact that men, more than women, are involved in extradomestic exchanges. In turn, these serve to establish reciprocal obligations and bonds outside the family and hence function as power bases. In her epilogue, Friedl addressed the status of women in the contemporary world, especially the United States. She argued that simply working for wages will not lead women to social equality with men, if those wages are used primarily for consumption within the household. If women are to become the equals of men, they must be employed in occupations high enough to enable them to distribute goods and services to persons outside the home, or their incomes must be great enough to be exchanged in business, political, or community contexts (1975:136). The primary goal for feminists from Friedl's perspective is, therefore, equality of employment opportunity at the highest levels.

HARRIS

In a very different vein, Marvin Harris (1978) argued that male supremacy is rooted in warfare, which in turn has resulted from population and resource pressures (see chapter 2). He clearly asserted, however, that "the fact that warfare and sexism have played and continue to play such prominent roles in human affairs does not mean they must continue to do so for all future time" (1978:66). He was convinced that this can change but offered no advice on how. The logical deduction from his perspective is that pacifism must be a major feminist goal. But peace cannot exist, according to Harris, in a world of population pressure and resource scarcity. Therefore, population control and the conservation and more equitable distribution of the world's resources would also have to be included as fundamental feminist goals.

SANDAY

Sanday's theory of male dominance (1981) focused on technologically simple societies, and her discussion of change was overwhelmingly directed at those environmental stresses and technological shifts that serve to *increase* the extent of male dominance (see chapter 2). She also addressed those mechanisms that serve to mitigate against increased male dominance under the same conditions. More pertinent to this chapter, in passing, Sanday noted some cases in which the balance of power shifted in favor of females under colonialism. This occurred in some areas of Africa where colonial administrations outlawed war. This resulted in greater trade opportunities for women and hence their greater access to wealth compared to male family members (1981:131). However, this explanation does not really flow from the logic of her own theory, which stressed the central importance of cultural configurations, sex-role plans, and origin myths — not economic and political variables.

In an epilogue, Sanday argued that we are still guided by religiously rooted symbols of the sexes, regardless of our supposed secularization. She ended by advocating that feminists retrieve those ancient Judeo-Christian symbols, which she amply documented, that once served to incorporate the feminine principle in these faiths. The logic of her theory suggests that in order to reduce gender inequality now, a new sex-role plan must become pervasive in society which is based more on an inner orientation stressing nurturance and cooperation. Her theory further suggests that such a change in cultural orientation needs to be rooted in and legitimated by a change in religious understanding, especially the creation myth.

The same emphasis on cultural variables informed Ortner's discussion (1974) of the causes of female subordination. Recall from chapter 2 that she argued that gender inequality is universal and rooted in the nature/female–culture/male dichotomy. By emphasizing the universality of female subordination, her theory left little room for a theoretically based strategy for change. She did, however, recognize throughout her essay that women are indeed involved in culture. It is the universal *perception* of their embeddedness in nature which she analyzed. She ended her discussion by calling for a change in cultural view and for the equal involvement of men and women in "projects of creativity and transcendence" (1974:87). Besides the vagueness of these goals, how they might be achieved cannot be deduced from this theory.

SUMMARY

The anthropological theories that have been reviewed have nothing to say about *how* change can take place—those that discuss change differ in their analyses of what is most critical to change. Like the Marxist-feminists, some anthropologists argued that the division of labor by gender constitutes the main target of change, especially childcare responsibilities. The other major theme in the anthropological tradition stresses the centrality of cultural variables. The focus of change from these perspectives is upon cultural, including religious, definitions.

ECLECTIC STRUCTURAL THEORIES

HOLTER

Holter's (1970) analysis of gender differentiation and stratification in contemporary industrial societies focused heavily on the ideological components that legitimate this form of ascriptive allocation. Recall from chapter 3 her assertion that for any ascriptively based system to survive, one or more of three conditions have to be met: people must believe (1) that there are innate differences between members of the different categories; (2) that the system of differentiation is God–given or natural; or (3) that system efficiency is enhanced. Obviously, then, one route to changing a system of gender differentiation and stratification is to undermine whichever of these beliefs legitimate it, a focus not unlike that of some anthropologists who urge change in cultural definitions.

Gender systems are vulnerable to attack in contemporary Western societies because, in general, such societies stress achievement as the primary basis for differentiation and stratification, according to Holter. Gender, as an ascribed basis, is thus contradictory to other central social values. The distribution of rewards by gender may be seen as violating standards of justice, which are rooted in achievement criteria (1970:33–4; 217). Holter also argued that whether or not a gender system continues to receive widespread support is a function of the balance of rewards and costs accrued by each sex, and whether promised rewards for conformity are in fact usually obtained. If there is persistent discrepancy between the promise and the reality, challenge is more likely. Challenge is also likely to occur if there is too great a discrepancy in the reward-level of the two sexes. Women must perceive such discrepancies and inequities if they are to act on that basis. For such perceptions to arise, however, women must consider it legitimate to compare themselves and their rewards to those of men. Such a comparison is precisely what the ideological underpinnings listed above tend to discourage.

Nonetheless, feminist movements have arisen in Western societies, at least among a minority of women, that reject the ideological underpinnings of gender-based ascription, make the relevant comparisons to men, and challenge the system. This minority is recruited from those upper-class women whose class and superior education have been discrepant with their gender status. Holter posited that such status discrepancy provides the prime motivation to challenge the ascribed system of gender differentiation (1970:39).

In 1970, Holter did not appear optimistic that the minority of feminists would grow substantially or that their challenge would result in substantial change; nonetheless, she offered a theory that included a logically consistent method of change. If the primary focus of attack is ideology, then consciousness raising constitutes a reasonable strategy for developing an attack on gender stratification. Moreover, Holter located the cadre of women capable of beginning the process of consciousness raising among those who experience status discrepancies.

CHAFETZ AND DWORKIN

The variable of status discrepancies assumed central importance in a theory I developed with my colleague Gary Dworkin. We sought to explain the conditions under which women become aware of their collective disadvantages and organize into a women's movement oriented to changing social structure in order to alleviate those inequities (Chafetz and Dworkin, 1986:chapter 3; also Chafetz and Dworkin, 1983). This was *not* a theory of change per se and contained no argument directly linking movement development to change. It is reasonable to suppose that where women's movements arise, and especially where they grow beyond a very small size, they are likely to have some impact on changing the structure of their societies in the direction of greater gender equality.

Our main thesis was that macrostructural changes emanating primarily from the process of industrialization, and including the related processes of urbanization and the growth of the middle class, produce a pool of women likely to experience certain social-psychological responses. It is from that pool that activists are drawn to create a women's movement. In turn, the greater the levels of change in the macrostructural variables, the larger the pool of affected women, and thus the larger the size of the women's movement.

We argued that the structural changes brought about by the process of industrial development serve to increase the nondomestic, public roles available especially to middle-class women (**role expansion**). The emphasis on middle-class women is because such movements, regardless of time or place, are overwhelmingly middle class in composition and especially in their leadership. Until the post-World War II era, such role expansion did not generally include employment roles for married middle-class women. Rather, women's roles expanded in premarital employment, social movement activism (e.g., temperance, peace, socialist, and nationalist movements), philanthropy, and voluntary social welfare work. As middle-class women become less encapsulated in the traditional domestic role, they begin to encounter **status/role conflicts**. By this we meant that others treat them according to traditional expectations of their gender, while their newly emerging roles prompt a desire for a new kind of response to them. As the number of women experiencing such conflict grows, given that they are spatially concentrated in the growing urban areas, many come into contact with one another. As they do, they begin to discuss their common problems and shift their comparative reference group from other women to men functioning in the same types of public roles. As they compare themselves with men, many will begin to develop a gender consciousness. This includes the perceptions thay they are unfairly treated and that it is the social system which is to blame. This consciousness then becomes the basis for the development of a women's movement oriented to system change. Such women are also apt to possess the resources necessary to mount a social movement, based both on their middle-class status and on the skills, knowledge, and networks acquired in their new public roles. In the absence of a politically repressive system that prevents social movement development, some of these women will form organizations that become the core of a women's movement. How large that movement grows depends on the size of the pool of affected women from which potential adherents can be drawn.

We argued that in the pre-World War II era, the goals and demands of women's movements were relatively conservative, focusing on issues of women's rights, such as educational opportunities, voting rights, and equal treatment under the law. Because married middle-class women were not in the labor force, early women's movement ideology typically accepted traditional gender definitions that focus priority on women's domestic and maternal obligations and men's economic obligations. The assumption of innate gender differences and separate gender spheres was largely unchallenged. They demanded change primarily in order to expedite the fulfillment of stereotypically feminine role obligations (1986:chapter 4).

The expansion of the labor force participation of married middle-class women occurred in response to fundamental economic changes that have taken place since the 1950s in the most highly industrialized nations. This new role expansion triggered a new wave of women's movements, which followed the same general process as earlier movements. The women's movements that have arisen since the late 1960s are ideologically far more radical in their demands. They reject all notions of gender-based separate spheres and demand not merely equality of formal rights and opportunities, but reproductive freedom, male involvement in domestic work, public child-care, and an end to stereotyped gender portrayals in the media and classroom (1986:chapter 5). We suggested that the more radical ideology results from the fact that role expansion for women in such societies has now reached the point where, regardless of marital status, women often participate in exactly the same range of roles as men, but not on equitable terms. The earlier women's movements resulted from partial role expansion, recent ones have been based on complete role expansion; early movements espoused a partial set of equity demands, recent ones a total set.

The extent to which change in the relative status of women results from movement activity, as opposed to being the product of the very same structural processes which we postulated produce women's movements, cannot be determined. The size to which such a movement grows is also not the only variable that might affect its success in realizing its goals. It is likely that the existence of a women's movement expedites and hastens change and that larger movements are more likely to meet with at least some success than smaller ones.

CHAFETZ

While my theory with Dworkin on the emergence of women's movements indirectly suggested how change might occur, it was my earlier theory, discussed in chapter 2, which implied what must change in order to reduce gender stratification. In that theory (Chafetz, 1984) I considered the independent variable **Level / Type of Technology** the single most important factor in generating a gender stratification system through its indirect but strong impact on the work organization variables. Because the theory is a systemic one, meaning that the variables are all interrelated, change in the degree of gender inequality can presumably come about by introducing change in any of the other variables comprising the theory. All variables in the theory, however, are not equally important: the work organization variables were considered the most important. Therefore, to be maximally effective, intervention would have to be either directed at those or at key independent variables that directly affect work organization. Secondarily, but nonetheless importantly, gender inequality can be reduced by altering aspects of family structure. The most effective targets of change for any given society would depend on the particular situation of that society in terms of the variables enumerated in the theory. In turn, to a substantial degree where a society is in terms of these other variables should be a function of its technological level. The theory is sufficiently eclectic that there are any number of specific intervention targets that could be deduced from it that should have some potential for reducing gender inequality. Change in gender stratification occurs naturally as a result of technological change, but not always in the direction of increased equality. To insure a direction toward increased equality would entail careful analysis of the likely results of any proposed change on the entire system of variables. From the discussion of my theory in chapter 3, one *unlikely* source of effective intervention is in social definitions, a stand which sets this theory in contradiction to a number of others (e.g., Sanday, Holter). My theory postulated the Marxian view that social definitions arise out of and reinforce economic and other structural phenomena. Where such definitions are changing, they are typically reflecting and buttressing — not causing — structural change, especially in the economy and family.

BLUMBERG

My emphasis on the centrality of economic variables is similar to that of Rae Blumberg. In the most recent statement of her macrotheory of gender stratification (1984) she did not discuss how societies can or do change in the direction of greater equality, but the logic of her theory readily lends itself to deductions about change. Her position that women's relative economic power is the most important determinant of a gender stratification system was discussed in chapter 2. Such economic power is primarily a function of women's **strategic indispensability** to productive work. Obviously, for women to achieve greater equality, they must first increase their contributions to their society's productive work (if it isn't already very high). But Blumberg made it very clear that, by itself, that will result in nothing. After all, slaves do almost all productive labor in slave-based societies. Women must, in addition, achieve greater strategic indispensability in their work, and Blumberg discussed a variety of variables that contribute to this (1984:57–62). Women will be easily replaceable, and therefore have low substitution costs at the margin and low strategic indispensability, if even as few as 5 to 15 percent are not employed but available for employment. Therefore, full employment for women, although perhaps a utopian vision in most contemporary societies, appears to be a very important goal. Less utopian is the possibility of control over technical expertise. Given substantial sex segregation of jobs, women already have considerable control over such expertise in some fields. Blumberg also argued that women can increase their power by organizing, which in turn is expedited when they do not work under close male supervision and do work cooperatively rather than competitively.

COSER

The emphasis on women's work roles is also apparent in the theories of Rose Coser. In the last chapter, her (1975) argument was reviewed that spatial restrictions on women reinforce both the gender and social stratification systems. For Coser, the displacement of women from the home, which requires childcare centers, is a critical variable in reducing gender inequality. If women were employed equally with men in prestigious occupations, they would be as free to travel as are men, and therefore to expand their role-sets and possibly enhance their individual status. It is not clear which needs to come first: childcare, occupational opportunity, or spatial mobility. The thrust of her essay was to suggest that the three are intimately interrelated, and therefore, simultaneous change in all is probably necessary. At any rate, Coser has been virtually alone in stressing the theoretical importance of spatial mobility in understanding women's status.

In her later paper with Rokoff (1982), Coser analyzed the ways in which the differing status/role obligations of women and men impact their occupational opportunities (see chapter 3). Their main contention was that women's relative disadvantage in the labor force reflects and reinforces the assumption that family, not work roles, constitute their first priority. Because of this, women are presumed to be risky as occupants of high status positions which require psychological commitment and a minimum of disruption due to absence. For these authors, the change required to equalize men's and women's opportunities is equity in family responsibility:

> If husbands were routinely expected to be as fully responsible for the management of disruptions in the family system as wives are now, it would become much more difficult to maintain the idea that higher-status professions have to be wary of women as potential disrupters of the routines of occupational life. (1982:52)

KANTER

In chapter 3 Kanter's theory (1977) of the structural components that reproduce gender inequality in formal work organizations was discussed. Those components—powerlessness, blocked opportunity, and tokenism—presumably affect people in similar ways, regardless of individual attributes.

However, they are confronted much more frequently by women than by men. In her concluding chapter, Kanter (1977:chapter 10) proposed a large number of concrete organizational changes designed to create a more humane working environment for all employees who confront such problems. They were also specifically directed at equalizing the statuses of men and women within the organization. I will confine this review to Kanter's general approaches and a few specifics most relevant to women since it is beyond the scope of this book to mention all of her suggestions.

Kanter suggested several specific strategies to enhance opportunities for employees in low-mobility jobs, especially clerical workers and secretaries. She also proposed more extensive horizontal mobility between jobs as an antidote for people facing blocked mobility. Given her definition of power in terms of resources that enable goal accomplishment, she argued that more people can be empowered if organizational hierarchies are flattened and decentralized, thereby permitting more autonomy to work units and individuals. In terms specifically of women's status relative to men, her most salient recommendations concerned eliminating tokenism. She argued for batch hiring of women, rather than one at a time. Perhaps more practically, she suggested the clustering of women within the organization's structure: "Women should be clustered in groups of sufficient numbers to be no longer identifiable as tokens, even if it means that some groups or departments or units or locales have none at all" (1977:282). She also encouraged the formation of women's networks and support groups to combat the problems that arise from numerical scarcity. Dominants, that is men, must be educated through training programs to understand the effects of tokenism on women. In all of these ways Kanter hoped to see the development of more humane, efficient, and sexually equalitarian organizations.

COLLINS

From a very different perspective, Collins's macrostructural theory (1975) located the source of male dominance in a strong sexual urge coupled with superior strength. However, this is often mitigated by economic and political structures. Collins argued that women have fared best in two kinds of societies. The first is nonsurplus-producing (simple technology) tribal societies, which have little stratification of any kind. In these cases, women's labor power produces most of the food and, in the absence of a surplus, men are little motivated to control and use their daughters as sexual property to bargain with other families. The second type is affluent market economies, such as the contemporary United States. With their own incomes, women are freed from parental control, which would use them as sexual property to be exchanged with other families. Women enter into their own bargains with men; nonetheless, this does not result in gender equality. Males still possess superior coercive power as well as superior economic resources. Collins concluded that "sexual stratification is not about to disappear" (1975:254).

While he was less that optimistic, his theory does logically suggest that the degree of gender inequality can be decreased—perhaps eliminated. To do so, male coercive power over females would have to be eliminated, presumably by strict enforcement of existing laws on wife abuse, sexual assault, and so on, and also by defining sexual coercion within marriage as legal rape. Second, as with many other theories already reviewed, women and men must become equal in their control over the economic resources of the society. Despite the biological basis of Collins's theory, social structural factors were introduced and posited to have sufficient power to all but eliminate the biological advantage of men.

Lipman-Blumen

Lipman-Blumen (1976) stressed the centrality not of male coercion but of their homosociality—their preference for other males—in her theory concerning how gender inequality is perpetuated (see chapter 3). She did not explicitly offer a theory of change, but hinted at some factors that must be changed. She mentioned that women's main resource to bind men to them has been children, but in turn children impede women's independent access to resources. Declining fertility rates were therefore explicitly mentioned as one road to increased equality. However, she discussed this in extreme terms that are unlikely to be relevant to the vast majority of women:

> When more women choose to remain nonparents, their ability to develop human capital in terms of education and work experience and their access to more responsible, higher-status and higher-income jobs should increase. (1976:21)

In addition, this assertion contradicts the central logic of her own theory, which mainly argued that women are *excluded* by homosocial males, not that they lack skills to compete effectively with them. There is no theoretical (or empirical) reason to believe that increasing women's human capital will automatically reduce gender inequality in significant ways.

She also argued that in crisis situations, such as wars, individuals previously excluded from various roles are allowed access to them and even deliberately recruited for them. However, there is considerable evidence that the status quo ante typically reemerges after the crisis is resolved. At any rate, a feminist program designed to bring about gender equality could scarcely predicate its program on awaiting (not to mention producing) a war or national calamity.

In terms of her own theory, the most important strategy would appear to be the production of homosociality among women, which Lipman-Blumen recognized as precisely what the feminist movement has done:

> Women are beginning to develop a new homosocial world of their own, turning to one another, rather than to men, for help in exchange relationships. There are indications of an emerging "new-girl network" analogous to the powerful "old-boy network" of the male world. (1976:18)

Implicit in this view is the assumption that the power of men resides primarily in their homosociality, which can be counteracted only by power rooted in a similar female consciousness and collective organization.

GIELE

In a rare example of a theory focused specifically on explaining change in the gender system, Janet Giele developed an evolutionary model (1978). This model is an adaptation of Neil Smelser's functional theory of the hierarchy of social controls which determine the order in which innovations are institutionalized. Giele delineated four ascending levels of social structure: (1) personality and role characteristics of individuals; (2) organizational characteristics of collectivities, such as families, firms, and schools; (3) institutional principles governing the major functional complexes of the society (e.g., the government, the economy, and the educational system); and (4) values and other major cultural themes on which the whole society is patterned (1978:14–15). She argued that this hierarchy appears to affect the selection of what topics become important at any given time in the change process. It is only when the highest level—that entailing societal values—is implicated that the overall structure is substantially changed. The impetus for ascending this hierarchy is, first and foremost, strains inherent within a society. However, forces external to the society operating on a global level and threatening the very survival of the society eventually come into play in producing change at the highest levels.

In more concrete terms, Giele argued that initially reform movements such as a women's movement focus on issues of personality and social roles. Policies and change strategies are oriented to enhancing women's educational and training opportunities and to reshaping women's personalities in order to "fit the available social slots" (1978:18). These efforts are somewhat successful in that some women gain access to jobs from which they had been barred by lack of qualifications. To the extent that inequities remain, the next efforts are directed at collectivities in an effort to achieve equality of results, not just expanded opportunities. The primary policy at this level is affirmative action. Again, if inequities persist, action is directed upward at institutional rules and goals: "Attempts are made to reform the basic institutional fabric so that the psychological orientation and occupational skills of women . . . are restored to proper balance with those of the dominant group [men]" (1978:17). Finally, continuing strain focuses efforts on changing the most general organizing principles of the culture and the symbol system such as language, gender stereotyping, and the dominance of such masculine values as mastery and domination over nature. An effort is made to replace these with a new emphasis on cooperation, sympathy, and vulnerability, which are values currently associated with femininity.

Movement from one level to the next, and therefore gender system change itself, is a function of the work done by women's movement members, scientists, and policymakers. Feminists function to point the way to change at all levels; they provide a will to foster change. Scientists provide information and theoretical bases to guide policy formation and implementation. Finally, policymakers "develop rules that express consensus on social purpose and permit change to be instituted" (1978:20). However, society is fundamentally resistant to change. At first, only changes at the lowest, least threatening levels are permitted. Broader changes do not occur until each major group comes to share certain common perceptions of problems and certain common values. Giele suggested that in a world of resource shortages, poverty and overpopulation in poor nations, and overconsumption in wealthy ones, there will be increased external pressure to change the gender system at the highest two levels. This will supplement internal pressure resulting from continuing inequities.

SAFILIOS-ROTHSCHILD

A final structural theory of gender change is found in a suggestive essay by Constantina Safilios-Rothschild (1979). She applied a conflict model, rooted in Marx's general theory of social change, to the issue of gender inequality. She assumed that men and women as social groups must engage in a conflict process if radical social change is to take place. The core of her theory pertained to the conditions that tend to enhance or depress the likelihood of conflict and thus of change.

She postulated first that the less the spatial and social segregation between the sexes, the more likely they are to come into conflict. Second, the greater the degree to which women have developed a collective consciousness of their disadvantage, the greater the degree of conflict with men at both the interpersonal and structural levels. Such structural conflict will occur through organized activism, while the interpersonal is an individual-level phenomenon. Third, she contended that the more women expect of men, the greater the probability of interpersonal conflict. Moreover, the more women opt for direct achievement for themselves, the higher both the interpersonal and structural levels of conflict with men. On the other hand, the more paternalistic and protective the discrimination against women, the lower the probability of conflict, until a social movement comes into existence and raises collective consciousness. Under conditions of paternalism, many women will prefer to maintain the protective legislation, policies, and practices that allow them to be dependent upon men. The result is that there is almost as much conflict between women as between men and women. Moreover, men can use such fragmentation among women to neutralize those who protest against the status quo, labeling them as deviants who betray their femininity. Finally, Safilios-Rothschild postulated that as discrimination becomes more subtle and informal (rather than overt and formal), conflict at the structural level diminishes, although it remains at the individual level. However, women's newly gained collective consciousness cannot help them in coping with conflictual confrontations with men on the interpersonal level.

Putting the various propositions into sequence, the following picture is suggested by the logic of Safilios-Rothschild's theory. Women begin to develop a collective consciousness of their deprivation on the basis of decreased gender segregation, with the result that structural and interpersonal conflict with men rises. This leads to some social change, which probably renders gender discrimination more subtle and covert. Moreover, the extent of change is limited by fragmentation among women themselves. Nonetheless, the changes that do occur may be sufficient to undermine the probability of continued structural conflict and therefore of more extensive change. While Safilios-Rothschild did not surrender her commitment to radical change, the logic of her formal theory renders extensive change unlikely — at least in the short- or medium-range future. At any rate, from this theoretical perspective, change of any degree requires conflict, which in turn requires collective consciousness by women. Concrete strategies for change would therefore be focused on consciousness raising and organizing women to engage in collective conflict with men, a strategy that is not different from the traditional Marxist emphasis on the development of working class consciousness and interclass conflict.

SUMMARY

What is most important to change in order to bring about gender equality, from the various eclectic structural perspectives? The most frequent answers echo those stressed in the earlier sections of this chapter: the nature of the gender division of labor; women's childcare responsibilities; women's opportunities to achieve equality with men in the labor force (Blumberg, Chafetz, Coser, Coser and Rokoff, Kanter, Collins). These aspects of work are tightly interwoven for many of the theorists. Like some of the anthropologists, Holter stressed the primary necessity of ideological or cultural definitional change, a stance which I explicitly rejected in my theory. The most complete attempt to explain gender–system change reviewed was offered by Giele, who suggested several ascending levels of targets, the ultimate one of which was also cultural values and themes. Finally, Collins was unique in focusing on the central need to curb male physical coerciveness.

Unlike the theories reviewed earlier in this chapter, several of the eclectic structural theories explicitly suggested how change might occur. Virtually all of these explanations focused on one or both of two typically related phenomena: the development of gender consciousness by women and the development of women's organizations devoted to pursuing women's interests, in adversarial relation to the institutions which support the status quo (Holter, Chafetz and Dworkin, Lipman-Blumen, Giele, Safilios-Rothschild). Two theories (Holter, Chafetz and Dworkin) explicitly attempted to explain how this process has been set in motion with reference to status discrepancies experienced by growing numbers of middle-class women as a result of broad societal changes.

EXCHANGE THEORY

Two Exchange theory accounts of gender stratification discussed in earlier chapters focused on the gender division of labor, and especially women's labor force opportunities, as the key to achieving gender equality.

PARKER AND PARKER

Parker and Parker (1979) argued that in technologically simple societies, biological differences between the sexes constitute the main basis for the division of labor (see chapter 2). That division of labor, however, is asymmetrical, requiring females to grant power and prestige to males in order to balance exchanges between the sexes. In their conclusion they argued that contemporary technology has rendered those biological differences irrelevant for determining the division of labor in society. They were confident that the sexual division of labor will break down, that differences in the qualities of male and female labor will tend to disappear. Indeed, a society which fails to do so

> may be seriously disadvantaged in evolutionary competition. The functional aspects of the myth of male superiority are becoming increasingly dysfunctional and even constitute a "drag" on the ability of society to exploit new sources of energy and creativity. (1979:303)

Their theory logically implies that as the division of labor approaches equality (symmetry), neither sex will be required to compensate the other with superior power or prestige in order to maintain exchange reciprocity (balance).

CURTIS

Curtis's (1986) social exchange approach to gender inequality within the family (see chapter 3) did not include an explicit discussion of social change. However, there are clear deductions that can be drawn from it. First, Curtis argued that a major underpinning of male power is male authority. Authority is defined in terms of agreement, both by its wielders and recipients, on the legitimate right of wielders to make binding decisions. Therefore, if large numbers of women deny men that automatic right, by definition authority will cease to exist. Other major power resources, especially economic, have accrued from the roles men play outside the family. Curtis's argument suggests that as married women enter the labor force, earn more equitable salaries, have more access to jobs entailing authority, and match their husbands in educational attainment, the power resources available to them within families should come to approximate those available to men. Social exchanges within the family should therefore become more equal, and in turn this should function to further increase gender equality in the market place (see Chafetz, 1980b for a similar argument).

FEMINIST NEO-FREUDIAN THEORIES

CHODOROW

Recall that Chodorow's feminist revision of Freudian theory (1978) argued that systems of gender inequality are reproduced by the fact that women function as the primary caretakers of infants and young children. This not only psychologically predisposes girls to want to grow up to mother, it creates boys who do not want to nurture children, and ultimately re-creates the entire gender stratification system. Since she rejected any notion that women's predisposition to mother is innate or biological in origin, there is nothing that absolutely precludes radical change in parental roles and therefore the system of gender stratification. Substantially increased paternal involvement, in fact equal parental involvement in early childhood caretaking, should, logically, result in the demise of gender inequality.

Chodorow discussed the strains and contradictions that have emerged around the mother role in recent decades in the United States (1978: Afterward). The widespread dissatisfaction resulting from such strains offers hope for the restructuring of parental roles. While advocating equal parental involvement and convinced that this is possible, Chodorow maintained that it is far from inevitable. Indeed, she also recognized that resistance to changes in the gender system is often strongest around women's maternal functions.

Beyond practical difficulties, there is a logical problem in Chodorow's approach to change in the system of gender inequality. From her perspective, the adult propensity and psychic wherewithal to nurture young children is established in early childhood, contingent upon the sex of the person (child) and caregiver. Because the vast majority of boys are now nurtured primarily by females, how can a generation of adult men be produced who will want and be able to effectively nurture young children? How does one break into the cycle, so convincingly portrayed by Chodorow, to begin equal parental involvement? Just as I argued earlier that her theory concerning the *reproduction* of inequality became circular when applied to the issue of the basic causes of gender inequality, its circularity is evident when we seek to understand how change might be possible. While men may indeed come to be more equally involved in parental tasks, and the results posited by Chodorow may come to pass, the logic of her own theory does not offer a mechanism by which this could occur.

KITTAY

Kittay's (1983) theory concerned womb envy, which, along with female subordination, she viewed as universal constants (see chapters 2 and 3). She adamantly rejected the idea that these can be reduced to biological fact, however. Rather, womb envy results from the fact that "sexual difference in procreative contributions is elaborated into a gender difference regarding the continued nurturance of the baby, once outside the womb" (1983:121). Therefore, although Kittay was sanguine about the prospects, it is possible to create a system of sex equality because it is possible to eliminate womb envy. To do so, in addition to understanding the substantial male role in procreation, boys must be strongly nurtured by their fathers from earliest infancy. Because womb envy is closely fused in the boy's mind with the special love and power he accords to his mother, he could transform, rather than repress, his childbearing wishes into nurturing ones, if he experienced such nurturance from his father. But, as in Chodorow's case, there is a logical problem: how do men who were reared by women, who presumably suffer womb envy, become nurturant fathers? It is a problem that Kittay recognized quite clearly.

RUBIN

Rubin attempted to revise and integrate the theories of Lévi-Strauss and Freud (explained in chapters 2 and 3 of this text). She argued that the exchange of women as marital partners is the basic cause of gender inequality. This exchange is rooted in the oedipal crisis, which is the mechanism by which youngsters internalize their appropriate gender, heterosexuality, and their culture's sexual rules and regulations (especially the incest taboo). Although she asserted that these processes have existed since the dawn of human society, Rubin did not think that they are immutable. Indeed, she argued that while the organization of sex and gender once had functions other than its own perpetuation (namely, the very organization of human society), it no longer does. Nonetheless, it continues in force.

Rubin pointed out that kinship has been stripped of its political, economic, educational, and organizational functions: "reduced to its barest bones — *sex and gender*" (1975:199). Given this, although human sexuality will always be subject to cultural forces, we today can liberate it from the straightjackets of the past. Her vision of such liberation "is one of an androgynous and genderless (though not sexless) society in which one's sexual anatomy is irrelevant to who one is, what one does, and with whom one makes love" (1975:204). Unfortunately, Rubin's only suggestions concerning how to produce such a utopia is a general reference to the need for political organization and activism. It is perhaps unarguable that the sex and gender system "will not wither away in the absence of opposition" (1975:203). Nonetheless, it is difficult to deduce from her analysis either specific targets of change or specific intervention strategies to produce such a totally revolutionary set of changes as those she proposed.

FLAX

Jane Flax (1981) attempted to combine Marxist-feminist and neo-Freudian feminist analyses of patriarchy and capitalism. She asserted that

> women's inferior status is rooted materially in the three interacting spheres central to human life: production, reproduction, and psychodynamics. . . . The material basis of women's oppression is *particular forms* of social organization which vary over time. (1981:124)

In the absence of radical change that transforms all three spheres, the sources of oppression may shift from sphere to sphere.

> Work would have to be transformed in at least four ways: 1) a redefinition of what counts as socially useful work [to include] . . . work traditionally done by women — caring for people and interpersonal relationships, beautifying personal environments, raising children and maintaining daily life; . . . 2) a redistribution of socially necessary work; 3) breaking down the division between

public and private; 4) a re-organization of work relations themselves . . . according to what will satisfy human needs [rather than
generate profits], both for services and for gratifying work.
(1981:131)

Were such changes to occur in the sphere of work, the growth and development of children would no longer be only women's work. In addition,
women would no longer be seen primarily as childrearers, only fit for employment which is an extension of that role. In turn, as childrearing becomes
more shared by parents and more vested in childcare centers, the gender-
specific psychodynamics which Chodorow analyzed will begin to disappear,
reinforcing the transformations in work and family.

SOCIALIZATION THEORIES

Taken together, the various theories that comprise the Socialization approach
suggest that gender identity is established in the early years of life by a complex and subtle set of mechanisms, many not within the control, or at least
the full control, of parents (e.g., media, peers, teachers). Moreover, being basic to self-identity, conceptions of gender are presumably resistant to substantial change in this theoretical tradition, as they are also in the neo-
Freudian. Finally, implicit in Socialization theories is the idea that the content
of gender-roles learned in childhood is likely to be quite traditional, even
when the parents are not necessarily traditional in their own roles. Given this
perspective, it is difficult to see where one could intervene to reduce gender
differentiation, which presumably constitutes a major prop for gender inequality.

CAHILL

Cahill's (1983) Symbolic Interactionist approach to the formation of gender
identity and the learning of gender appropriate behaviors exemplified this
problem. The focus of his theory was on the importance of parental and peer
expectations and responses. Recall that I concluded that discussion by asserting that to the extent that a child's parents and those of her or his peers express traditional notions of gender, the child would do so as well. Cahill
noted in passing, however, that this approach is readily adaptable to less
traditional social interactional and developmental patterns. That is, nontraditional parents, combined with peers whose parents are also nontraditional,
will tend to rear children whose concept of gender, for self and others, is nontraditional. As a change strategy, however, this presents a classic chicken-or-
egg-first quandary. If our core self-identity is formed in early childhood, including our conceptions of gender, how do we produce a first generation of

nontraditional parents? Clearly, one must look outside of this theoretical approach for the sources of such change. Once a significant number of nontraditional parents emerges, this perspective leads to the conclusion that new gender conceptions could be transmitted intergenerationally, presumably affecting the system of gender stratification. To do so, parents must structure the home environment, including books and television viewing, and their own interactions with their children to reinforce nontraditional gender behaviors. They must also carefully control the peers with whom their children interact, which is perhaps more important and far more difficult. At best, such a change strategy is slow, indirect in its effects on the macro system of gender inequality, and fraught with potentially subverting mechanisms due to lack of parental control over the environment outside the home.

Katz

Phyllis Katz (1979) has taken a different approach, while nonetheless remaining within the general socialization framework. She began with three assumptions: that sex role socialization occurs over the entire lifespan; that at different life stages, the cognitive and social tasks associated with sex roles that are to be mastered differ; and that the social influences on sex-role development associated with each stage differ. She divided the life span into three levels, childhood, adolescence, and adulthood, each of which is further divided into two or three stages (e.g., infancy, preschool, and grade school for the childhood level). Primary influences include parents, peers, teachers, and spouses, depending on the level and stage. While for most women, the traditional sex-role script is reinforced at each level and stage, change has obviously occurred among many women. Such change can occur because some levels and stages are more open to it than others. In general, the preschool period is not very susceptible to change because stereotyped thinking is the rule at this stage of cognitive development. During school age, peers become the most powerful influence, and they too constitute a generally conservative influence. However, adolescent peers are far less conservative, often rebellious, offering an opportunity to alter one's sex role. Young adulthood, the period when people are dealing with issues of marriage and parenthood, is a time when people enter delayed modeling of their parents, and is usually quite conservative. If their parents were nontraditional, this is the point where it shows up in their offspring, not earlier. Women can respond to changing opportunities, argued Katz, modifying their roles and self-concepts, because as girls they were taught a huge number of skills, many of which it was assumed they would not use. By using a life-cycle perspective, Katz was better able to provide an opening for change to occur than those who focus only on the early childhood acquisition of gender identity.

LEVER AND COSER

While the various socialization theories, with the exception of Katz, presented arguments that appear logically to preclude widespread change, they nonetheless identify several specific elements in childhood learning that make logical targets of change. Two examples taken from theories reviewed in chapter 3 can demonstrate this. Janet Lever (1976) analyzed the role of play in socializing children for adult gender roles, thereby contributing to the maintenance of the gender status quo. The change target which flows in a straightforward manner from this approach is for parents and schools to encourage boys and girls to engage in the play activities that are usually sex-typed for the other. Lever also suggested that adults structure nonplay activities that can teach each sex that which the other learns via play. Rose Coser (1986) employed a cognitive developmental approach that argued that social and physical restraints placed by parents on girls limit the development of their cognitive skills. In turn, this limitation makes them best fit for an adult life lived largely within the confines of the domestic sphere. The target of change that emanates from this is straightforward: girls need to have opportunities equal to those of boys to move away from the house physically and to interact socially with a wide variety of people. Girls must take on more complex role-sets and become less focused on a small number of intimate relationships. Coser believed that this has already begun to occur in the United States. How or why such changes have begun cannot be adequately understood, however, from her perspective.

EVERYDAY LIFE APPROACHES

Everyday Life theories stress the manner by which people develop shared meanings and perceptions of social reality through interaction. When the feminist versions of this perspective were examined in chapter 3, a common thread that ran through many was the idea that gender inequality is reproduced because males have superior power to define situations, values, and gender norms. It can be anticipated, then, that the focus of change urged by theorists in this tradition is primarily on the power to create cultural definitions: language, evaluative standards, definitions of femaleness, of gender itself.

KESSLER AND MCKENNA

In chapter 3, Kessler and McKenna's (1978) ethnomethodological account of the gender attribution process was discussed. The point was made that underpinning systems of gender inequality are a set of cultural assumptions that define reality as comprised of two and only two genders, into one of which all people fit, and a social process by which we attribute gender to others. Kessler and McKenna argued that as long as we define people as fitting into one of only two mutually exclusive categories of male or female, there will be scientific and lay searches for differences, and differences will be found. When there are dichotomies it is difficult to avoid evaluating one in relation to the other, thus providing a firm foundation for discrimination. From this perspective, the elimination of gender inequality requires that "gender, in all of its manifestations *including the physical*, is seen as a social construction" (1978:164). People must see that this way of perceiving reality is just that: one, but not the only means of understanding reality. In fact, they argued that except for those few times in life when a person wishes to reproduce, and must therefore identify self and at least some others as sperm or egg carriers, there need be no differentiation among people on any of the dichotomies which gender implies (1978:166).

FERGUSON

Ferguson's (1980) symbolic interactionist approach to understanding how systems of gender inequality are maintained stressed male power to define both specific interactional situations and societal standards and norms (the generalized other) (see chapter 3). She also engaged in a lengthy discussion of the meaning of liberation from a Meadian Symbolic Interaction perspective. She claimed that the concept refers to a dialectic between freedom, or defining one's own situation, and compassion, or taking the perspective of the other. For women, they are already adept — perhaps too adept — at the latter. Change toward greater gender equality involves their acquisition of the power to define themselves (1980:172).

To gain such power, women must gain legal and economic independence. However, she argued, that is not sufficient; it is not the same as enabling them to reject the psychological burden of the male-defined view of themselves. To do so, women must have a diverse number of roles available to them so that they can become aware of alternatives and are in contact with diverse reference groups. She thought that American women have already accomplished this to a considerable extent. Ferguson further suggested that changes in the structure of families toward more extended and communal ones could broaden children's self-definitions. Finally, consciousness-raising, once a characteristic practice of women's liberation movement groups, can be very instrumental in the process of attaining self-definition for women. I might add that from Ferguson's perspective, the influx of feminist scholars into the humanities and social sciences, along with the spread of women's studies programs, would have to be considered important tools in gaining the power of self-definition for women. Likewise, images of women in the media that depict them as self-defining would be important. Finally, Ferguson was only too aware of obstacles to the changes she proposes and of the dilemmas and contradictions that would result if both sexes came to equally share freedom and compassion.

SCHUR

In a manner similar to Ferguson, Labeling theorist Schur (1984) argued that because males possess far more power than females, they are able to define and impose their definitions of deviance on women. He argued that men benefit psychologically, socially, and in economic terms from the devaluation of women, and in turn, such devaluation creates a self-fulfilling prophecy that supports the status quo. However, since deviance is a social construction, it is amenable to conscious efforts at change. Schur suggested that feminists must begin by recognizing

> that the routine objectification of females—a response that has become for most men virtually a matter of habit—constitutes a major obstacle that must be surmounted. . . . In particular, the prevailing visual imagery of women . . . in pornography [and] also in respectable advertising may have to be a central feminist target . . . .(1984:240)

He recognized that because superior male social power undergirds their power to define situations and norms, women must have equal access to socioeconomic and political power. But such power is a necessary prerequisite, not the ultimate goal. It must be used to change definitions of femaleness. Schur also suggested that other, collective female efforts, such as consciousness-raising groups, assertiveness training, and medical self-help programs for women, are important in helping women to overcome devaluation. In short, from his perspective, the basic mechanism that sustains gender incquality is definitional power, so the ultimate change required is in the definition of femaleness and gender norms. For that purpose, other forms of power are required.

FEMINIST LINGUISTS

The feminist linguists discussed in chapter 3 argued that men and women use language differently, and in turn this difference both expresses and reinforces gender inequality. Two very different kinds of suggestions for social change emanate from this. One the one hand, it can be argued that women should maintain their pattern of language usage, that what needs to be changed is the androcentric view that assesses the feminine pattern as inferior to the masculine. Such change would probably require a total cultural and social alteration of the gender system, first, by which females would lose their devalued status. In turn this implies equality in power. This was the view taken by McConnell-Ginet (1978). On the other hand, it can be argued that women must assume a more assertive language usage, one more akin to the masculine style. While arguing for male change as well, so that both sexes would use both styles, the thrust of Lakoff's work (1975) emphasized this second approach. However, Lakoff more modestly recognized that social change usually creates language change, not vice versa; that at most, language change may slowly and indirectly influence attitudinal change. The two approaches to change suggested by linguists mirror a broader normative issue of great concern to contemporary feminists: to what extent should women become manlike in seeking equality, versus to what extent should the negative assessment of feminine qualities be the focus of change efforts?

SUMMARY AND CONCLUSIONS

At the outset of this chapter two issues were presented: What needs to change to produce gender equality? How can such change come about? There is no paucity of answers to the first question. Virtually all theories that address issues related to gender stratification imply, if they don't explicitly suggest, the major target(s) of change. In this chapter, answers to this question that reflect every general theoretical tradition discussed in any of the preceding three chapters have been reviewed. However, few theories have ventured suggestions concerning how change can or does occur, and even fewer have generated logically consistent answers to the second question.

Theories from almost every perspective have focused on the division of labor by gender as a fundamental target for change. Such change, in turn, encompasses two closely related alterations. On the one hand, women must be totally integrated into central, powerful economic roles (e.g., the Marxist-feminists, Friedl, Chafetz, Blumberg, Coser, Collins, the Exchange theorists, Flax, and most of the Everyday Life theories). On the other hand, women must be relieved of the primary responsibility for domestic, and especially childrearing tasks, by making them social labor or through equal paternal involvement (e.g., the Marxist-feminists, Schlegel, Rosaldo, Chafetz, Coser, Coser and Rokoff, the Freudian feminists). The reduction of maternal responsibility was viewed as both a prerequisite for economic equality and, by some theorists, as a direct prerequisite for changing the gendered personalities that underlie systems of gender inequality.

The other major theme apparent in theories from a variety of perspectives focused on the critical importance of changing ideology, including religious and cultural definitions and expectations (e.g., Sanday, Ortner, Holter, Giele, the Socialization and Everyday Life theories). The Everyday Life theories (e.g., Ferguson, Schur, and the linguists) argued that the legal and especially economic power of men and women must first be equalized in order for the genders to be equal in their ability to define situations, cultural images and evaluations, which are the fundamental inequities upon which they focused. Other aspects of culture, such as play forms, the mass media, and educational tools and practices, constituted the major targets of change for Socialization theories (e.g., Cahill, Lever).

Theoretically based, logically consistent approaches to the issue of how change can or does occur were to be found primarily among the more macro-level theories. The micro theories tend to run into problems of circular reasoning in their discussions of change, regardless of specific perspective. This occurs because they argue that gender inequality is rooted in the childhood creation of gender differences, which become stable adult traits. How, then, are nontraditional adults to be produced who can rear children in a different way? Even among the macro theories, however, many failed to suggest answers to this question, while most of the answers that were provided lacked depth and detail. Virtually all of the change strategies reviewed focused on one or more of three interrelated processes: (1) the development of gender consciousness (Marxist-feminists, Holter, Chafetz and Dworkin, Safilios-Rothschild, Ferguson, Schur); (2) the organization of women into their own groups, networks, collectivities (Marxist-feminists, Chafetz and Dworkin, Blumberg, Kanter, Lipman-Blumen, Giele, Safilios-Rothschild, Rubin); and (3) entering into conflict relations with men and dominant social institutions (Marxist-feminists, Safilios-Rothschild, Rubin). Where the central goal of change concentrated on cultural definitions and ideology, consciousness raising was as far as the theories typically went in suggesting mechanisms for change. Organization and conflict are processes aimed primarily at changing the distribution of resources (e.g., political or economic power).

The three processes just enumerated, taken together and divorced from the specificity of gender, represent Marx's general theory of social change, as outlined in chapter 1. For Marx, consciousness development, the first step, arises because of an increased concentration of, and interaction between, members of an oppressed class. Through contact with one another they come to understand their oppression and its structural causes. Macrostructural changes in technology and the economy were posited as triggering the process. Three of the theories reviewed in this chapter (Holter, Chafetz and Dworkin, Safilios-Rothschild) explicitly devoted attention to the issue of why women have recently come to develop gender consciousness, and to organize on that basis into conflict-oriented women's movements. These theories, like Marx's, rooted the process in broadscale socioeconomic changes. Such changes have served to decrease women's segregation from men and from one another, to foster status discrepancies or conflict for women, and in this manner to encourage the development of gender consciousness and organization among women.

Changing Systems of Gender Inequality 155

Understanding the change process can be potentially very useful in practical terms, to the extent that such understanding can inform both the setting of intermediate goals on the road to full gender equality, and the choice of strategies for feminist activists. Such understanding may serve to generate public policy ideas as well. It should be apparent that the various theoretical approaches vary considerably in both their potential practical applicability and in the specific advice they generate. Clearly, gender inequality is deeply embedded in all aspects of social and cultural life, and in the very personalities of most societal members. It might appear that everything has to change more or less simultaneously in order for gender equality to be realized. This is a daunting prospect.

I suggested in the opening chapter that virtually all of the theories covered in this book have some useful role to play in moving toward a more complete understanding of gender systems. What is required now is a sustained effort toward theoretical synthesis, which crosses the micro-macro levels as well as the various traditions within each level. Such a synthesis would provide a more intellectually satisfying understanding of gender. It should also enhance our ability to devise maximally useful ways of applying our activist energies and resources to the job of eliminating gender inequality. A theoretical synthesis that enables us to pinpoint those aspects of social life that are both of critical importance in sustaining the gender status quo and potentially amenable to pressure by feminists could reduce the sense that the task before us is apparently overwhelming. I remain committed to the goal of gender equality, optimistic that it will be approached in coming decades, and convinced that feminist activists can be most effective when informed by an empirically supported, theoretical understanding of the gender system.

REFERENCES

Acker, Joan
    1973   "Women and Social Stratification: A Case of Intellectual Sexism." *American Journal of Sociology* 78(January): 936–45.

Barron, R. D. and G. M. Norris
    1976   "Sexual Divisions and the Dual Labour Market," pp. 47–69 in Diana Leonard Barker and Sheila Allen (eds.), *Dependence and Exploitation in Work and Marriage*. London: Longman.

Bell, Colin and Howard Newby
    1976   "Husbands and Wives: The Dynamics of the Deferential Dialectic," pp. 152–68 in Diana Leonard Barker and Sheila Allen (eds.), *Dependence and Exploitation in Work and Marriage*. London: Longman.

Bennholdt-Thomsen, Veronika
    1984   "Towards a Theory of the Sexual Division of Labor," pp. 252–70 in Joan Smith, Immanuel Wallerstein, and Hans Dieter Evers (eds.), *Households and the World Economy*. Beverly Hills, CA: Sage.

Blumberg, Rae Lesser
    1984   "A General Theory of Gender Stratification," pp. 23–101 in Randall Collins (ed.), *Sociological Theory*. San Francisco: Jossey-Bass.

Bologh, Roslyn Wallach
    1984   "Feminist Social Theorizing and Moral Reasoning on Difference and Dialectic," pp. 373–93 in R. Collins (ed.), *Sociological Theory*. San Francisco: Jossey-Bass.

Breines, Wini
  1986   "The 1950s: Gender and Some Social Science," *Sociological Inquiry* 56(1): 69–92.
Cahill, Spencer
  1983   "Reexamining the Acquisition of Sex Roles: A Symbolic Interactionist Approach," *Sex Roles* 9(1): 1–15.
Chafetz, Janet Saltzman
  1980a   "Toward a Macro-level Theory of Sexual Stratification and Gender Differentiation," in S. McNall and G. Howe (eds.), *Current Perspectives in Social Theory I*. Greenwich, CT: JAI Press.
  1980b   "Conflict Resolution in Marriage: Toward a Theory of Spousal Strategies and Marital Dissolution Rates," *Journal of Family Issues* 1(3): 397–421.
  1984   *Sex and Advantage: A Comparative, Macro-Structural Theory of Sex Stratification*. Totowa, NJ: Rowman and Allanheld.
  1985   "Marital Intimacy and Conflict: The Irony of Spousal Equality," *Free Inquiry in Creative Sociology* 13(November): 191–96.
Chafetz, Janet Saltzman and A. Gary Dworkin
  1983   "Macro and Micro Processes in the Emergence of Feminist Movements: Toward a Unified Theory," *Western Sociological Review* 14: 27–45.
  1986   *Female Revolt: Women's Movements in World and Historical Perspective*. Totowa, NJ: Rowman and Allanheld.
Chodorow, Nancy
  1974   "Family Structure and Feminine Personality," pp. 43–66 in Michelle Zimbalist Rosaldo and Louise Lamphere (eds.), *Women, Culture, and Society*. Stanford, CA: Stanford University Press.
  1978   *The Reproduction of Mothering: Psychoanalysis and the Sociology of Gender*. Berkeley, CA: University of California Press.
  1979   "Mothering, Male Dominance, and Capitalism," pp. 83–106 in Zillah Eisenstein (ed.), *Capitalist Patriarchy and the Case for Socialist Feminism*. New York: Monthly Review Press.
Collier, Jane F. and Michelle Z. Rosaldo
  1981   "Politics and Gender in Simple Societies," pp. 275–329 in Sherry B. Ortner and Harriet Whitehead (eds.), *Sexual Meanings: The Cultural Construction of Gender and Sexuality*. New York: Cambridge University Press.
Collins, Randall
  1975   *Conflict Sociology: Toward an Explanatory Science*. New York: Academic Press.
Constantinople, Anne
  1979   "Sex-Role Acquisition: In Search of the Elephant," *Sex Roles* 5(2): 121–33.

Cook, Judith A. and Mary Margaret Fonow

1986 "Knowledge and Women's Interests: Issues of Epistemology and Methodology in Feminist Sociological Research," *Sociological Inquiry* 56(1): 2–29.

Coser, Rose Laub

1975 "Stay Home, Little Sheba: On Placement, Displacement, and Social Change," *Social Problems* 22(April): 470–80.

1986 Cognitive Structure and the Use of Social Space," *Sociological Forum* 1(Winter): 1–26.

Coser, Rose Laub and Gerald Rokoff

1982 "Women in the Occupational World: Social Disruption and Conflict," pp. 39–53 in R. Kahn-Hut, A. Kaplan Daniels, and R. Colvard (eds.), *Women and Work*. New York: Oxford University Press. First published 1971 in *Social Problems* 18(Spring): 535–54.

Cucchiari, Salvatore

1981 "The Gender Revolution and the Transition from Bisexual Horde to Patrilocal Band," pp. 31–79 in S. Ortner and H. Whitehead (eds.), *Sexual Meanings: The Cultural Construction of Gender and Sexuality*. New York: Cambridge University Press.

Curtis, Richard

1986 "Household and Family in Theory on Inequality," *American Sociological Review* 51(April): 168–83.

Eisenstein, Zillah

1979 "Developing a Theory of Capitalist Patriarchy and Socialist Feminism," and "Some Notes on the Relations of Capitalist Patriarchy," pp. 5–55 in Zillah Eisenstein (ed.), *Capitalist Patriarchy and the Case for Socialist Feminism*. New York: Monthly Review Press.

Engels, Friedrich

1972 *The Origin of the Family, Private Property and the State*. New York: Penguin Books. Translated by Alick West. First published 1884.

Farganis, Sandra

1986 "Social Theory and Feminist Theory: The Need for Dialogue," *Sociological Inquiry* 56(1): 50–68.

Ferguson, Kathy

1980 *Self, Society, and Womankind*. Westport, CT: Greenwood Press.

Fishman, Pamela

1982 "Interaction: The Work Women Do," pp. 170–80 in R. Kahn-Hut, A. K. Daniels, and R. Colvard (eds.), *Women and Work: Problems and Perspectives*. New York: Oxford University Press.

Flax, Jane.
1981   "A Materialist Theory of Women's Status," *Psychology of Women Quarterly* 6(Fall): 123–36.
Fox, Greer Litton
1977   " 'Nice Girl': Social Control of Women through a Value Construct," *Signs* 2(4): 805–17.
Friedl, Ernestine
1975   *Women and Men: An Anthropologist's View.* New York: Holt, Rinehart and Winston.
Giele, Janet Zollinger
1978   *Women and the Future: Changing Sex Roles in Modern America.* New York: The Free Press.
Gilligan, Carol
1982   *In a Different Voice.* Cambridge, MA: Harvard University Press.
Goffman, Irving
1959   *The Presentation of Self in Everyday Life.* Englewood Cliffs, NJ: Prentice-Hall.
1977   "The Arrangement between the Sexes," *Theory and Society* 4(3): 301–31.
Guttentag, Marcia and Paul Secord
1983   *Too Many Women? The Sex Ratio Question.* Beverly Hills, CA: Sage.
Haavind, Hanne
1984   "Love and Power in Marriage," pp. 136–67 in Harriet Holter (ed.), *Patriarchy in a Welfare Society.* Oslo: Universitetsforlaget.
Harris, Marvin
1978   *Cannibals and Kings: The Origins of Cultures.* London: Collins.
Hartmann, Heidi
1979   "Capitalism, Patriarchy, and Job Segregation by Sex," pp. 206–47 in Zillah Eisenstein (ed.), *Capitalist Patriarchy and the Case for Socialist Feminism.* New York: Monthly Review Press.
1984   "The Unhappy Marriage of Marxism and Feminism: Towards a More Progressive Union," pp. 172–89 in Alison Jaggar and Paula Rothenberg (eds.), *Feminist Frameworks: Alternative Theoretical Accounts of the Relations between Women and Men.* New York: McGraw-Hill.
Henley, Nancy
1977   *Body Politics: Power, Sex, and Nonverbal Communication.* Englewood Cliffs, NJ: Prentice-Hall.
Holter, Harriet
1970   *Sex Roles and Social Structure.* Oslo: Universitetsforlaget.
1972   "Sex Roles and Social Change," pp. 331–43 in Constantina

Safilios-Rothschild (ed.), *Toward a Sociology of Women*. Lexington, MA: Xerox College Publishing.

Horner, Mattina
1972   "Toward an Understanding of Achievement-Related Conflicts in Women," *Journal of Social Issues* 28: 157–75.

Kanter, Rosabeth Moss
1977   *Men and Women of the Corporation*. New York: Basic Books.

Kasper, Anne
1986   "Consciousness Re-Evaluated: Interpretive Theory and Feminist Scholarship," *Sociological Inquiry* 56(1): 30–49.

Katz, Phyllis
1979   "The Development of Female Identity," *Sex Roles* 5(2): 155–78.

Kessler, Suzanne and Wendy McKenna
1978   *Gender: An Ethnomethodological Approach*. New York: John Wiley and Sons.

Kittay, Eva Feder
1983   "Womb Envy: An Explanatory Concept," pp. 94–128 in Joyce Trebilcot (ed.), *Mothering: Essays in Feminist Theory*. Totowa, NJ: Rowman and Allanheld.

Lakoff, Robin
1975   *Language and Woman's Place*. New York: Harper Colophon Books.

Lever, Janet
1976   "Sex Differences in the Games Children Play," *Social Problems* 23(April): 478–87.

Lewis, Michael and Marsha Weinraub
1979   "Origins of Early Sex-Role Development," *Sex Roles* 5(2): 135–53.

Lipman-Blumen, Jean
1976   "Toward a Homosocial Theory of Sex Roles: An Explanation of the Sex Segregation of Social Institutions," *Signs* 1(Spring): 15–31.

Lockheed, Marlaine
1985   "Sex and Social Influence: a Meta-Analysis Guided by Theory," pp. 406–29 in Joseph Berger and Morris Zelditch, Jr. (eds.), *Status, Rewards and Influence*. San Francisco: Jossey-Bass.

Mayo, Clara and Nancy Henley
1981   "Nonverbal Behavior: Barrier or Agent for Sex Role Change?" pp. 3–13 in Clara Mayo and Nancy Henley (eds.), *Gender and Nonverbal Behavior*. New York: Springer-Verlag.

McConnell-Ginet, Sally
1978   "Intonation in a Man's World," *Signs* 3(Spring): 541–59.

Mead, George Herbert
1934   *Mind, Self and Society*. Chicago: University of Chicago Press.
Meeker, Barbara and Patricia Weitzel-O'Neill
1985   "Sex Roles and Interpersonal Behavior in Task-oriented Groups," pp. 379–405 in Joseph Berger and Morris Zelditch, Jr. (eds.), *Status, Rewards and Influence*. San Francisco: Jossey-Bass.
Merton, Robert K.
1957   *Social Theory and Social Structure*. Glencoe, IL: The Free Press.
Mies, Marcia
1983   "Towards a Methodology for Feminist Research," in G. Bowles and R. Klein (eds.), *Theories of Women's Studies*. Boston: Routledge & Kegan Paul.
Millman, Marcia and Rosabeth Moss Kanter
1975   *Another Voice: Feminist Perspectives on Social Life and Social Science*. Garden City, NY: Anchor Books.
Oakley, Ann
1974   *The Sociology of Housework*. New York: Pantheon Books.
Ortner, Sherry B.
1974   "Is Female to Male as Nature is to Culture?" in Michelle Z. Rosaldo and Louise Lamphere (eds.), *Woman, Culture and Society*. Stanford, CA: Stanford University Press.
Ortner, Sherry and Harriet Whitehead
1981   "Introduction: Accounting For Sexual Meanings," pp. 1–27 in Sherry Ortner and Harriet Whitehead (eds.), *Sexual Meanings: The Cultural Construction of Gender and Sexuality*. New York: Cambridge University Press.
Parker, Seymour and Hilda Parker
1979   "The Myth of Male Superiority: Rise and Demise," *American Anthropologist* 81(2): 289–309.
Rebecca, Meda, Robert Hefner, and Barbara Oleshansky
1976   "A Model of Sex-Role Transcendence," pp. 90–97 in Alexandra Kaplan and Joan Bean (eds.), *Beyond Sex-Role Stereotypes: Readings toward a Psychology of Androgyny*. Boston: Little Brown & Co.
Rosaldo, Michelle Z.
1974   "Woman, Culture, and Society: A Theoretical Overview," in Michelle Rosaldo and Louise Lamphere (eds.), *Women, Culture and Society*. Stanford, CA: Stanford University Press.
Rosenblum, Karen
1986   "The Conflict between and within Genders: An Appraisal of Contemporary American Femininity and Masculinity," *Sociological Inquiry* 56(Winter): 93–104.
Rubin, Gayle
1975   "The Traffic in Women: Notes on the 'Political Economy' of

Sex," in Reyna Reiter (ed.), *Toward an Anthropology of Women*. New York: Monthly Review Press.

Sacks, Karen

1974 "Engels Revisited: Women, the Organization of Production, and Private Property," pp. 207–22 in Michelle Zimbalist Rosaldo and Louise Lamphere (eds.), *Woman, Culture, and Society*. Stanford, CA: Stanford University Press.

Safilios-Rothschild, Constantina

1979 "Women as Change Agents: Toward a Conflict Theoretical Model of Sex Role Change," pp. 287–301 in J. Lipman-Blumen and J. Bernard (eds.), *Sex Roles and Social Policy*. Beverly Hills, CA: Sage.

Sanday, Peggy

1974 "Female Status in the Public Domain," pp. 189–206 in Michelle Zimbalist Rosaldo and Louise Lamphere (eds.), *Woman, Culture, and Society*. Stanford, CA: Stanford University Press.

1981 *Female Power and Male Dominance: On the Origins of Sexual Inequality*. Cambridge: Cambridge University Press.

Sattel, Jack

1976 "The Inexpressive Male: Tragedy or Sexual Politics," *Social Problems* 23(April): 469–77.

Schlegel, Alice

1977 "Toward a Theory of Sexual Stratification" and "An Overview," pp. 1–40 and 344–57 in Alice Schlegel (ed.), *Sexual Stratification: A Cross-Cultural View*. New York: Columbia University Press.

Schur, Edwin

1984 *Labeling Women Deviant: Gender, Stigma, and Social Control*. New York: Random House.

Sokoloff, Natalie

1980 *Between Money and Love: The Dialectics of Women's Home and Market Work*. New York: Praeger.

1981 "Theories of Women's Labor Force Status: A Review and Critique," *Current Perspectives in Sociological Theory* 2: 153–86.

Stacey, Judith and Barrie Thorne

1985 "The Missing Feminist Revolution in Sociology," *Social Problems* 32(April): 301–16.

Sutherland, Elyse and Joseph Veroff

1985 "Achievement Motivation and Sex Roles," pp. 101–28 in V. O. Leary, R. Unger, and B. Wallston (eds.), *Women, Gender, and Social Psychology*. Hillsdale, NJ: Lawrence Erlbaum Associates.

Vogel, Lise

1983 *Marxism and the Oppression of Women: Toward a Unitary Theory*. New Brunswick, NJ: Rutgers University Press.

References 163

Ward, Kathryn
    1984   *Women in the World-System: Its Impact on Status and Fertility*. New York: Praeger.
West, Candace, and Don Zimmerman
    1977   "Women's Place in Everyday Talk: Reflections on Parent-Child Interaction," *Social Problems* 24(June): 521–29.
    1987   "Doing Gender," *Gender & Society* 1: 125–51.
Westcott, Marcia
    1979   "Feminist Criticism of the Social Sciences," *Harvard Educational Review* 49: 422–30.

INDEX

investment policies and, 129
labor division and, 29, 30, 31, 32,
33, 34, 36, 37, 42, 45, 49, 116
legitimatizing, 71
Marxist Feminist Theories, 28–38,
128–131
maternal responsibility and, 154
mechanisms of, 3, 51
patriarchy and, 30, 31, 68
population pressure and, 46, 48
prestige structure and, 44, 48
religious support, 53, 133
reproduction of, 114
resource shortage and, 46, 48
sex learning, 90, 93, 95, 97, 99, 101,
102, 106, 107, 110, 112, 146
social life spheres, 41
technology and, 54, 59, 133, 137
urbanization effects, 136
work activities and, 52
World Systems Theory, 117
Gender norms, 114
Gender perception, 102, 134, 149
Gender relations, 5
Gender segregation, 143
Gender socialization, 95, 97, 99, 101,
102
Gender stratification, 28, 42, 48, 49,
50, 51, 54, 57, 139
Anthropological System, 38–51,
131–134
Eclectic Structural Theories, 117–120
gender differentiation result, 118
Marxist-Feminist Theories, 115–117
social consequences, 115–125
space use and, 118, 139
systems, 28, 57
Gender Systems:
change in, 127–156
maintenance of, 67–114
Eclectic Structural Theories, 70–89
Marxist-Feminist Theories, 68–70
reproduction of, 67–114
Eclectic Structural Theories, 70–89
Marxist-Feminist Theories, 68–70
Generational replacement, 31, 32, 34,
42, 53
Giele, Janet, 142, 145
Gilligan, Carol, 24
Global Assembly Line, 36
Goffman, Irving, 19, 107, 123

Guttentag, Marcia, 72

Harris, Marvin, 46
Hartmann, Heidi, 68, 116, 130
Hegel, Georg F.W., 7
Henley, Nancy, 105
Holter, Harriett, 73, 75, 118, 134
Homans, George, 25
Homosociality, 76, 141
Horner, Mattina, 101
Human capital, 100
Human Capital Theories, 100–101

Idealism, 7
Ideological hegemony, 78
Ideology:
and gender identity, 53, 134
gender inequality and, 154
In A Different Voice, 24
Industrialization, gender inequality
effects, 135
Infanticide, female, 46, 47
Infrastructure, 7
Interactional Approach, 120
Interpretive Theory, 112
Investments, 25
Isolation, domestic, 70

Kanter, Rosabeth, 84, 139
Kasper, Anne, 112
Katz, Phyllis, 150, 151
Kelley, Harold, 26
Kessler, Suzanne, 102, 108, 151
Kinship, 49, 56, 62, 94, 148
Kittay, Eva, 60, 93, 122, 147
Kohlberg, Lawrence, 24
Kuhn, Manfred, 18, 19

Labeling Theory, 19, 110
Labor:
gender-based division, 63
markets, 82, 83
middle-class participation, 136, 137
necessary, 32, 33, 34
sexual division of, 29, 30, 31, 32, 33,
34, 36, 37, 42, 45, 49, 53, 58,
132, 145
strategic indispensability, 56, 138
social, 29, 30, 34
surplus, 32, 33, 34
Lakoff, Robin, 105, 114

THE BOOK'S MANUFACTURE

Feminist Sociology
was typeset at
Stanton Publication Services, Inc.
Minneapolis, Minnesota.
The typeface is Gill Sans Light.
Printing and binding were done by
Arcata Graphics, Kingsport, Tennessee.
Cover design and text design
were done by John B. Goetz,
Design & Production Services Co., Chicago